HOUSE B

The Complete Home Style and Shopping Directory

Edited by Libby Norman

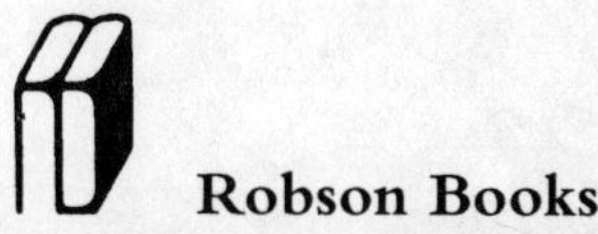

Robson Books

First published in Great Britain in 1997 by Robson Books Ltd, Bolsover House, 5–6 Clipstone Street, London W1P 8LE

British Library Cataloguing in Publication Data
A catalogue record for this title is available from the British Library

ISBN 1 86105 138 7

Edited by Libby Norman
Additional research by Becky Baxter, Lisette Mitchiner, Tania Smith

Although every effort has been made to give the correct contact information for the companies listed, it is possible that some details may have changed since this directory was published. If you're having trouble tracking down the company you want, contact the House Beautiful Enquiry Line on 0171 312 3906.

Typeset by Pitfold Design, Hindhead, Surrey
Printed in Great Britain by Creative Print & Design (Wales), Ebbw Vale, South Wales

CONTENTS

INTRODUCTION

The Complete Home Style and Shopping Directory from *House Beautiful* is the essential source book for your home. We've gathered together vital addresses to cut the legwork out of tracking down the look you want – whether you're making a major purchase like a kitchen or searching for budget fabric, traditional paint colours or unusual accessories. The book is divided into 12 easy-to-use chapters and includes both the major names and smaller suppliers and manufacturers, as well as useful sources of advice and tips to help you make the right choice. All the companies mentioned can supply you with a brochure, catalogue or details of your nearest local stockist or store. Happy shopping!

1 • KITCHENS

Your kitchen is a practical work area, but it's as prone to fashion as any other room in the house. In recent years, practical laminates and traditional wood have been joined by high-tech designs from Germany and Italy and, more recently, simple Shaker styles in bold colours. While it's perfectly possible to spend a fortune creating the look you want, budget and flatpack kitchen companies offer well-designed ranges at excellent prices. We've given starting prices for units wherever possible (please note that these are intended as a guideline only), and most companies listed here can supply a brochure or recommend you to a local dealer. If you don't want to rip your kitchen out and start again, you can always revamp by replacing doors, changing worktops and buying a new sink.

Kitchen Specialists Association

Many kitchen showrooms are members of the Kitchen Specialists Association. To join, they must have traded successfully for at least two years and demonstrated that they can provide a complete design, supply and installation service to an approved standard. All members also pay into a bond used to fund a deposit protection scheme – this means you won't lose your deposit if you order a kitchen from a KSA member which subsequently ceases trading. The association can also act as an arbitrator if you have a complaint about a KSA member. Contact the KSA's helpline on 01905 726066 or write to The Kitchen Specialists Association, FREEPOST WR716, Worcester WR1 1BR.

Budget and Flatpack Kitchens

B&Q

Portswood House, 1 Hampshire Corporate Park, Chandler's Ford, Hants SO53 3YX
Call 0500 300 150 for your nearest store

Budget to medium-price DIY kitchens. Installation available. Free planning. Base units from around £30/1,000mm

Crosby Kitchens

Holden Ing Way, Spring Ram Business Park, Birstall, West Yorkshire WF17 9AE
01924 424492

Large range of flatpack kitchens in laminate and wood. Installation available through retailer network. Base units from around £60/1,000mm

Gower Furniture

Holmfield Industrial Estate, Halifax, West Yorkshire HX2 9TN
01422 246201

Selection of laminate and wood designs. Planning and installation through retailers. Drawer base units from around £50/1,000mm

Graham Group

96 Leeds Road, Huddersfield, West Yorkshire HD1 4RH
01484 537366

Builders merchants with budget flatpack kitchens. Free planning. Installation available through retailers. Prices on application

Homebase

Call 0645 801 800 for your nearest store

Wide range of DIY flatpack kitchens. Installation available. Free planning. Base units from around £25/1,000mm

Ikea

2 Drury Way, North Circular Road, London NW10 0TH
0181 208 5600
Branches at Croydon, London Brent Cross, Lakeside Thurrock, Birmingham, Warrington, Leeds and Gateshead

Stylish flatpack kitchens. Free planning. Installation available.
Base units from around £60/600mm (inc 1 door and 2 shelves)

MFI Furniture Centres

Southon House, 333 The Hyde, Edgware Road, London NW9 6TD
0181 200 8000

Hygena flatpack range. Free planning. Installation available.
Base units from around £50/1,000mm (Hygena)

Moben Kitchens

MKD Holdings, Cornbrook, 2 Brindley Road, Old Trafford, Manchester M16 9HQ
0161 872 2422

Full range of kitchens supplied and fitted by Moben. Prices on application

Now Kitchens

Units A1–A3, Red Scar Industrial Estate, Longridge Road, Preston, Lancashire PR2 5NA
01772 7038383

Laminate and wood flatpack kitchens. Prices on application

Ram Kitchens

Holden Ing Way, Spring Ram Business Park, Birstall, West Yorkshire WF17 9AE
01924 424492

Flatpack budget kitchens. Planning and installation through retailers.
Base units from around £50/1,000mm

Wickes Building Supplies

120–138 Station Road, Harrow, Middlesex HA1 2QB
Call 0500 300328 for brochures and stores

A favourite of the building trade that's also open to the public. Good-value DIY kitchens. Free planning available on higher-priced Caernarvon range. Base units from around £20/1,000mm

---

Standard Measurements

Most kitchen companies supply fittings in standard widths. The narrowest are usually 200mm wide and increase in 100mm widths up to 600mm for single cupboards and 1200mm for units with double doors. Wall cupboards are generally not more than 300mm deep, while floor cupboards can be either 500mm or 600mm deep. The standard height for worksurfaces is 900mm, but this can usually be raised or lowered by adjusting a plinth on the base unit.

New for Old

Fitting replacement doors or worktops on to existing carcasses can be a cost-effective option if you want to update your kitchen without ripping everything out and starting again. Many DIY stores supply doors separately, or try the following specialists:

Birch Joinery

Call 01947 605624 for details

Unpainted and painted doors in MDF, wood and wood with stained-glass panels. Made-to-measure service

Façades

Freepost BD2406, Keighley, West Yorkshire BD20 5BR
01274 511234

Made-to-measure wooden kitchen doors and worktops

Frederick of Wood Green

387 High Road, London N22 4JA
0181 888 8164

Worktops in laminates and solid wood. Cut-to-size and mitre service. Non-standard lengths and widths available

Handmade Interiors

Call 01442 832891

Country-style doors

James Mayor Furniture

Call 0121 643 8349 for brochures

Made-to-order doors supplied unpainted, primed or painted

Mr Kitchen

Call 01622 814811 for brochures

Wide range of styles available, from raw MDF doors ready for painting to solid wood doors. Also supplies worktops

The Kitchen Door Company

Call 0161 654 6288 for details

Shaker-style, hand-painted and made-to-measure doors

The Replacement Kitchen Door Company

Call 01708 865386 for details

Made-to-measure wooden doors. Glass-fronted cabinets also available, plus made-to-match service for single doors

Mid-price and Luxury Kitchens

Allmilmo

80 Mersey Way, Thatcham, Berkshire RG18 3DL
01635 868181

Modern, colourful kitchens from Germany. Free planning. Installation available. Base units from around £250/600mm

Alno

Unit 10, Hampton Farm Industrial Estate, Hampton Road West, Hanworth, Middlesex TW13 6DB
Call 0181 898 4781 for local dealers

Contemporary designs from Germany and Pastoral Collection. Free planning. Installation available. Drawer base units from around £370/1,000mm

Andrew Macintosh

462-464 Chiswick High Road, London W4 5TT (showroom)
0181 995 8333

Hand-painted kitchens. Free planning. Installation available. Drawer base units from around £300/600mm

Ashley Stocks Furniture

The Studio, Units 9-10, Parkfield Trading Estate, Culvert Place, London SW11 5BA
0171 627 1222

Hand-made painted and lacquered wood kitchens. Free planning. Installation available. Prices on application

Bernstein Group

Silburn House, Great Bank Road, West Horton, Bolton BL5 3XY
01942 840840

Misty and Four Seasons brands. Planning and installation through retailers. Drawer base units from around £150/500mm

Boffi

Alternative Plans, 9 Hester Road, London SW11 4AN
0171 228 6460

High-tech Italian designs incorporating stainless-steel. Free planning. Installation available. Base units from around £220/600mm

Brookmans Design Group

Fairholme Works, Jawbone Hill, Oughtibridge, Sheffield
S30 3HN
0114 286 2011

Hand-made wooden kitchens. Paint finishes available. Free planning and estimates. Installation available. Drawer base units from around £330/600mm

Chalon

Hambridge Mill, Hambridge, Somerset TK10 0BP
01458 252374

Range of kitchens including freestanding pieces and paint effects

Bulthaup Kitchens

37 Wigmore Street, London W1H 9LD
0171 495 7220

High-tech designs from Germany. Installation available. Drawer base units from around £500/600mm

Christians

1 Pillory Street, Nantwich, Cheshire CW5 5BZ
01270 623333

Custom-made traditional wood kitchens. Free planning. Installation available. Prices on application

Cotteswood Kitchens

Station Road, Chipping Norton, Oxfordshire OX7 5HN
01608 641858

Traditional wood kitchens. Planning, design and installation available. Base units from around £250/600mm

C P Hart

Newnham Terrace, Hercules Road, London SE1 7DR
0171 902 1000

Modern and traditional hand-painted kitchens (33 ranges). Free planning. Installation available. Complete kitchens around £8,000

Crabtree Kitchens

The Twickenham Centre, Norcutt Road, Twickenham, Middlesex TW2 6SR
0181 755 1121

Custom-made and hand-painted wood kitchens. Drawer base units from around £470/500mm

Crown

Eddington Lane, Herne Bay, Kent CT6 5TR
01227 372217

Fitted kitchen furniture. Drawer base units from around £230/600mm (including five drawers)

Cuisine Bonnet

10–12 Bromley Road, Beckenham, Kent BR3 5JE
0181 658 0271

French kitchens in farmhouse and contemporary styles. Prices on application

Derek Pegrum Designs

The Old Brewery, Durweston, Blandford, Dorset DT11 0QE
01258 453987

Traditional and Shaker designs. Free planning. Installation available. Drawer base units from around £200/600mm

Hygrove Kitchens

152–154 Merton Road, London SW19 1EH
0181 543 1200

Hand-made painted or solid wood kitchens. Free planning. Installation available. Drawer base units from around £300/600mm

In-toto

Wakefield Road, Gildersome, Leeds, West Yorkshire LS27 7JZ
0800 252271

German Wellman kitchens and traditional British designs. Free planning. Installation available. Drawer base units from around £150/600mm

J C Hatt

Hartlebury Trading Estate, Hartlebury, Worcestershire
DY10 4JB
01299 251320

Wood and laminate designs. Free planning. Installation available. Prices on application

John Franklin Kitchens

The Beckery, Glastonbury, Somerset BA6 9NX
01458 834435

Traditional and contemporary British kitchens. Free planning. Installation available. Base units from around £220/500mm

John Lewis of Hungerford

Park Street, Hungerford, Berkshire RG17 0EA
01488 682066

Bespoke kitchens and lower-price Artisan range. In-store design and installation available for Artisan range. Base units from around £180/600mm

Johnson & Johnson Furniture

Unit 12–19, Guinness Road Trading Estate, Trafford Park, Greater Manchester M17 1SB

Custom-made country-style and painted kitchens. Prices on application

Kitchen Art

5–6 The Centre, The Broadway, Farnham Common, Buckinghamshire SL2 3PP
01753 646631

Custom-made designs. Prices on application

Magnet

Royd Ings Avenue, Keighley, West Yorkshire BD21 4BY
01535 661133

Selection of wood and laminate designs. Free planning. Installation available. Base units from around £170/1,000mm

Mark Wilkinson Furniture

Overton House, Bromham, Chippenham, Wiltshire SN15 2HA
01380 850004

Traditional British wood kitchens. Installation available. Prices on application

Martin Moore

36 Church Street, Altrincham, Cheshire WA14 4DW
0161 928 2643

Designers and makers of hard-wood, antique timber, painted finishes and Shaker styles. Installation available. Drawer base units from around £440/600mm

Miele

Fairacres, Marcham Road, Abingdon, Oxfordshire OX14 1TW
01235 554455

Colourful German kitchens. Free planning. Installation available. Prices on application

Naturally Wood

3 Twyford Road, Bishops Stortford, Hertfordshire CM23 3JL
01279 755501

Custom-made hardwood and timber kitchens. Free planning. Installation available. Prices on application

Nicholas Turner

Oldwell Studio, 58 High Street, Shaftesbury, Dorset SP7 8AA
01747 855044

Hand-made kitchens. Free initial quotation and design. Installation available

Paula Rosa

Water Lane, Storrington, West Sussex RH20 3DS
01903 743322

British wood and wood-effect kitchens. Free planning. Installation through retailer. Drawer base units from around £130/600mm

Poggenpohl Group

Silbury Court, 368 Silbury Boulevard, Milton Keynes, Buckinghamshire MK9 2AF
01908 247600

Modern German designs. Free planning. Installation through retailers. Prices on application

Pyram

286–288 Leigh Road, Leigh-on-Sea, Essex SS9 1BW
01702 480660

French traditional and modern designs. Free planning. Installation available. Drawer base units from around £120/600mm

Rational UK

24–28 Crossway House, High Street, Bracknell, Berkshire
RG12 1DA
01344 55800

Custom-made country style kitchens. Prices on application

Rhode Design

65 Cross Street, London N1BB
0171 354 9933

Good range of painted kitchens

Robinson & Cornish

Southay House, Oakwood Close, Barnstaple, Devon EX31 3NJ
01271 329300

Traditional custom-made designs. Free planning. Installation available. Drawer base units from around £650/600mm

Roundel Design

Flishinghurst Orchards, Chalk Lane, Cranbrook, Kent
TN17 2QA
01580 712666

Bespoke traditional designs. Planning, design and installation available. Drawer base units from around £300/600mm

Simon Taylor Furniture

Rowsham Road, Bierton, Aylesbury, Bucks HP22 5DZ
01296 88207

Custom-made traditional and contemporary designs. Free planning. Installation available. Prices on application

Smallbone of Devizes

105–109 Fulham Road, London SW3 6RL
0171 589 5998

Bespoke kitchens. Full design and installation. Kitchen starting price from around £7,000

Underwood Kitchens

Lawn Farm Business Centre, Grendon Underwood, Buckinghamshire HP18 0QX
01296 770043

Bespoke traditional designs. Planning and installation available. Drawer base units from around £300/600mm

Watts & Wright

The Woodworks, Bentley Road North, Walsall, West Midlands WS2 0DF
01922 22247

Hand-made kitchen furniture. Free planning. Installation available. Drawer base units from around £300/600mm

Wellmann UK

Wakefield Road, Gildersome, Leeds, West Yorkshire LS27 7JZ
0113 252 0154 (see In-toto)

Woodstock Furniture

4 William Street, London SW1X 9HL
0171 245 9989

Custom-made wood kitchens. Free planning. Installation available. Base units from around £400/600mm

Zeyko

The Business Design Centre, 52 Upper Street, London N1 0QH
0171 288 6123

Laminates and wood in traditional and modern finishes. Free planning. Installation available. Base units from around £190/600mm

Sinks

Whether you want a traditional Belfast sink or a made-to-measure model in stainless-steel, you can find a supplier:

Architectural Wall & Floor

Unit 3, Premier Mill, Begonia Street, Darwen, Lancashire BB3 2DR
01254 873994

Made-to-measure traditional sinks, including Belfast and combination range of styles

Aston Mathews

141–147 Essex Road, London N1 2SN
0171 226 7220

Wide range of sizes and styles in stainless-steel, ceramic or enamelled cast iron

Brass & Traditional Sinks

Devauden Green, Chepstow, Gwent NP6 6PL
01291 650738

Round or rectangular brass sinks, as well as ceramic Belfast and French farmhouse styles. Nationwide delivery

Frederick of Wood Green

387 High Road, London N22 4JA
0181 888 8164

Sinks in granite, quartz, corian and stainless-steel. Wide variety of designs and sizes

GEC Anderson

Oaken Grove, Shire Lane, Hastoe, Hertfordshire HP23 6LY
01442 826999

Stainless-steel sinks made to measure in any size and shape. Nationwide delivery

Appliances

AEG

Call 01635 572720 for brochures and stockists

Ariston

Merloni House, 3 Cowley Business Park, High Street, Cowley, Uxbridge, Middlesex UB8 2AD
0800 393140

Asko

Crown Domestic Appliances, Old Bank Buildings, 2 Coventry Street, Stourbridge DY8 1EP
01384 444244

Bosch

Old Wolverton Road, Wolverton, Milton Keynes, Buckinghamshire MK12 5PT
Call 01233 211500 for brochures

Creda

Blythe Bridge, Stoke-on-Trent, Staffordshire ST11 9LJ
01782 388388

Electrolux

101 Oakley Road, Luton, Bedfordshire LU4 9QQ
01582 585858

Hoover

Call 01685 721222 for brochures and stockists

Hotpoint

Call 0541 506070 for brochures and stockists

Indesit

Merloni House, 3 Cowley Business Park, High Street, Cowley, Uxbridge, Middlesex UB8 2AD
01895 858200

Miele

Fairacres, Marcham Road, Abingdon, Oxfordshire OX14 1TW
01235 554455

Neff UK

Grand Union House, Old Wolverton Road, Wolverton, Milton Keynes, Buckinghamshire MK12 5PT
01908 328354 (brochureline 0990 133090)

Panasonic

Panasonic House, Willoughby Road, Bracknell, Berkshire RG12 4FT
0990 357357

Parkinson Cowan

Call 01635 521313 for brochures and stockists

Smeg UK

Corinthian Court, 80 Milton Park, Abingdon, Oxfordshire
OX14 4RY
01235 861090

Stoves

Stony Lane, Prescot, Merseyside L35 2XW
0151 426 6551

Tricity Bendix

55–77 High Street, Slough, Berkshire SL1 1DZ
0990 805805

Whirlpool

PO Box 45, 209 Purley Way, Croydon CR9 4RY
0181 649 5000

White-Westinghouse

Corinthian Court, 80 Milton Park, Abingdon, Oxfordshire
OX14 4RY
01235 861090 (for American appliances)

Zanussi

55-77 High Street, Slough, Berkshire SL1 1DZ
0990 140140

Kitchen Ranges

Aga

Aga-Rayburn, PO Box 30, Ketley, Telford, Shropshire TF1 4DD
01952 642000. For local distributor call 0345 125207

Fuel: Gas (natural and LPG), oil or solid fuel and off-peak electricity
Colours: Blue, green, jade, cream, black, red, white, claret, emerald
From around £3,600 plus delivery and assembly

Belling

Belling Appliances, Talbot Road, Mexborough, South Yorkshire S64 8AJ
01709 579902

Fuel: Electric or dual-fuel (gas hob, electric oven)
Colours: Green, blue, red
From around £1,500 plus delivery and assembly

Bosky

UA Engineering, Canal Street, Sheffield S4 7ZE
0114 2738803

Fuel: Solid fuel, oil or gas
Colours: White, caramel
From around £1,500 plus delivery and fitting

Elmira Cook's Delight

Euroheat Distributors, Unit 2, Court Farm Business Park, Bishops Frome, Worcestershire WR6 5AY
01885 490474

Fuel: Gas or electric
Colours: White, black, almond, two-tone
From around £3,800

Esse

Ouzedale Foundry Company, PO Box 4, Long Ing,
Barnoldswick, Colne, Lancs BB8 6BN
01282 813235

Fuel: Wood, peat, solid fuel, oil or gas (natural or LPG)
Colours: White, charcoal, gold, mink, cornflower, Oxford blue, Buckingham green, classic green, cranberry, cream
From around £1,300

Fourneaux Morice

Euroheat Distributors, Unit 2, Court Farm Business Park,
Bishops Frome, Worcestershire WR6 5AY
01885 490474
Fuel: Gas or electric
Colours: Black, claret, blue, green, grey, white
Price: From around £4,500

Franco-Belge

ACR Distribution, PO Box 70, Knowle, West Midlands
B93 0EX
0121 706 8266

Fuel: Wood, coal, peat or oil
Colours: White, amber
From around £2,300

Nobel

Country Cookers, Bruff Works, Bush Bank, Suckley,
Worcestershire WR6 5DR

Fuel: Oil or gas
Colours: Blue, green, burgundy, ivory, black
From around £2,500

Rayburn

Aga-Rayburn, PO Box 30, Ketley, Telford, Shropshire TF1 4DD
01952 642000. For local distributor call 0345 125207

Fuel: Gas, oil, solid fuel or multi-solid fuel
Colours: Sable, dark blue, red, white, dark green, cream Wedgwood, emerald, jade, claret
From around £2,350

Rosieres

Maurice Lay, Fourth Way, Avonmouth, Bristol BS11 8DW
0117 982 3721

Fuel: Gas
Colours: White, black
From around £1,950

Stanley

Abbey Road, Wrexham Industrial Estate, Wrexham LL13 9RF
01978 664555

Fuel: Oil, solid fuel or gas (natural or LPG)
Colours: Claret, red, blue, green, black, mink, oyster, white
From around £2,800 plus delivery and fitting

Wamsler

Euroheat Distributors, Unit 2, Court Farm Business Park, Bishops Frome, Worcestershire WR6 5AY
01885 490474

Fuel: Oil or multi-fuel
Colours: White, shaded Havana
From around £2,250

Renovated Agas and Rayburns

Country Cookers specializes in renovated ranges and has a network of local distributors. Agas start at around £2,500 and come with a three-year parts guarantee. Rayburns cost from around £1,750 and come with a one-year guarantee. Call 01886 884262

---

2 • BATHROOMS

It may be the most functional room in the house, but your bathroom is also a retreat. That means you need to combine fittings that are hardwearing enough to stand up to repeated onslaughts from water and steam with extra touches that make it a place where you can relax and enjoy a long hot soak. White remains the safest choice for fittings because it doesn't date and gives you plenty of flexibility with your colour scheme. Look out though for the return of coloured suites in bold blues, greens and aquas.

Fittings

Armitage Shanks

Armitage, Rugeley, Staffordshire WS15 4BT
01543 490253

Bathroom fittings, showers and brassware

Aston Mathews

141–147 Essex Road, London N1 2SN
0171 226 7220

Large range of cast-iron baths, sinks, taps and mixers, WCs, ceramic shower trays, showers and accessories

B&Q

0181 466 4166 for your nearest store

Full range of bathroom fittings and accessories

Bath Craft

331 Devizes Road, Salisbury, Wiltshire SP2 9JN
01722 338999

Reconditioned cast-iron roll-top baths and re-enamelling service for existing fittings

Connections by Graham

96 Leeds Road, Huddersfield HD1 4RH
01484 537366

Bathroom suites, furniture, showers, floor and wall tiles, brassware, accessories and heated towel rails. Planning service available

C P Hart & Sons

Newnham Terrace, Hercules Road, London SE1 7DR
0171 902 1000

German Duker suites, acrylic and stainless-steel fittings, brassware, taps, accessories and heated towel rails

Dolphin Fitted Bathrooms

Bromwich Road, Worcester WR2 4BD
01905 748500

Complete bathrooms, including tiles, accessories and flooring

Doulton Bathroom Products

Lawton Road, Alsager, Stoke-on-Trent, Staffordshire ST7 2DF
01270 410026

Bathroom suites

Heritage Bathrooms

Heritage House, Princess Street, Bedminster, Bristol BS3 4AG
0117 9639762

Traditional bathrooms, brassware, bathroom furniture and accessories

Ideal Standard

National Avenue, Kingston-upon-Hull HU5 4HS
01482 346461

Bathroom fittings, furniture, showers and accessories

Jacob Delafon

Unit 1, Churchward, Southmead Park, Didcot, Oxon OX11 7HB
01235 510511

Bathroom suites

Koralle

Coventry Point, Market Way, Coventry CV1 1EB
01203 257212

Suites, accessories and tiles

Qualitas Bathrooms

Hartshorne Road, Woodville, Swadlincote, Derbyshire DE11 7JD
01283 550550

Full range of bathroom fittings and accessories

Saniflo

Freepost, PO Box 6, Burlingford, Herts SG9 9DR

WCs installed using small-bore pipework that makes them suitable for most rooms

Sanitan

Silverdale Road, Silverdale, Stoke-on-Trent ST5 6EL
01782 717175

Bathroom fittings

Shires Bathrooms

Beckside Road, Bradford, West Yorkshire BD7 2JE
01274 521199

Traditional bathroom designs in acrylic and vitreous china. Accessories

Simply Bathrooms

Unit 2, Felnex Industrial Estate, 190 London Road, Hackbridge SM6 7EL
0181 773 5000

Complete range of bathroom products, including baths, showers, tiles, lighting and accessories from 50 manufacturers. Design and installation service. Mail-order catalogue available. Curtains and blinds. Retail and wholesale

Texas Homecare

Beddington House, Wallington, Surrey SM6 0HB (0181 784 7200)
0645 801800 for your nearest store

Full range of bathroom fittings and accessories

Twyfords

Lawton Road, Alsager, Stoke-on-Trent, Staffordshire ST7 2DF
01270 879777

Bathroom suites

Vernon Tutbury

Silverdale Road, Newcastle-under-Lyme, Staffordshire ST5 6EL
01782 710755

Bathroom fittings

Villeroy & Boch Bathrooms

267 Merton Road, London SW18 5JS

Bathroom fittings and tiles

Vitra

121 Milton Park, Abingdon, Oxfordshire OX14 4SA
01235 820400

Bathroom fittings, tiles and accessories

Showers

Aqualisa

The Flyers Way, Westerham, Kent TN16 1DE
01959 561720 (for a brochure)

Showers and accessories

Aqualona Products

High Cross Centre, Fountayne Road, London N15 4QW
0181 801 4461

Shower curtains, shower screens and enclosures, massage kits, shower heads and hoses

Daryl Industries

Alfred Road, Wallasey, Wirral L44 7HY
0151 605 1549 (brochures 0151 606 5000)

Standard and bespoke shower enclosures and bath screens

Gainsborough Showers

Fifers Lane, Norwich NR6 6XB
01603 787171

Showers and accessories

Grohe

1 River Road, Barking, Essex IG11 0HD
0181 594 7292

Hansgrohe

Unit D17, Sandown Park Trading Estate, Royal Mills, Esher, Surrey KT10 8BL
01372 465655

Showers, cabinets, brassware and accessories

Matki

Freepost (BS7214), Yate, Bristol BS17 5PL
01454 322888

Shower doors, surrounds and shower trays

Mira Showers

Cromwell Road, Cheltenham, Gloucestershire GL52 5EP
01242 221221

Showers and accessories

Nordic Showers

Holland Road, Fairview Estate, Oxted, Surrey RH8 9BZ
01883 732400 (brochures 01883 716367)

Shower and bath screens, shower trays, fitted steam systems for Turkish steam baths and saunas

Powered Showers

Stoves, Stoney Lane, Prescot, Merseyside L35 2XW
0151 426 6551

Showers and accessories

Showeristic

Unit 10, Manor Industrial Estate, Flintshire, Clwyd CH6 5UY
01352 735381

Non standard and made-to-measure shower enclosures

Showerlux

Sibree Road, Coventry, West Midlands CV3 4EL
01203 639400 (brochures 01203 882505)

Basins, pedestal cabinets, shower screens/enclosures and trays, baths, mirrored cabinets and accessories

Teuco

Suite 314, Business Design Centre, 52 Upper Street, London N1 0QH
0171 704 2190

Whirlpool baths, multi-function showers, hydro showers and hydro steam

Triton

Shepperton Park, Caldwell Road, Nuneaton, Warwickshire CV11 4NR
01203 344441

Showers and accessories

Furniture and Accessories

Alibert

40 St Andrews Square, Berry Hill Industrial Estate, Droitwich Spa, Worcestershire WR9 9AB
01905 795796

Full range of bathroom furniture and fittings

Black Country Heritage

Britannia House, Mill Street, Brierley Hill, West Midlands DY5 2TH
01384 480810

Traditional-style accessories, including shaving mirrors and toothbrush holders. Mail order available

Christies

0800 192192 (for brochures and showrooms)

Fitted bathroom furniture

House of Brass

45–47 Milton Street, Nottingham NG1 3EZ
0115 9475430

Brass bathroom taps and accessories. Mail order available

Ikea

Branches at Croydon, London Brent Cross, Lakeside Thurrock, Birmingham, Warrington, Leeds and Gateshead
0181 208 5600

Bathroom cupboards, shelves, sinks and accessories

Imperial Towel Rails

Orbital 5, Orbital Way, Cannock, Staffordshire WS11 3XW
01543 574724

Heated towel rails

Keith Gray & Co

Great Priory Farm, Panfield, Braintree, Essex CM7 5BQ
01376 324590

Bespoke vanity units and bathroom cabinets

Keuco

Berkhamsted House, 121 High Street, Berkhamsted, Hertfordshire HP4 2DJ
01442 865220

Mirror cabinets, modular bathroom furniture and accessories

Market Square (Warminster)

Wing Farm, Longbridge Deverill, Warminster, Wiltshire
BA12 7DD
01323 644041

Ready-to-install pine bath panels

McFadden Cabinetmakers

Unit 3, Lymore Gardens, Bath BA2 1AQ
01225 310593

Bathroom furniture, including vanity units, panelled baths and wall cabinets in oak, maple, cherry and sycamore

Metlex

Shepperton Business Park, Caldwell Road, Nuneaton, Warwickshire CV11 4NR
01203 344441

Chrome, plate, ceramic and gold-effect accessories, bathroom cabinets and towel warmers

Myson

Call 0345 697509 for brochure

Heated towel rails

Rhode Design

137–139 Essex Road, London N1 2SN
0171 354 9933

Unpainted and painted MDF bathroom cabinets

Stiffkey Bathrooms

Stiffkey, Norfolk NR23 1AJ
01328 830084

Bathroom accessories in traditional designs. Mail order available

The Imperial Bathroom Company

Unit 2, Stag Industrial Estate, Oxford Street, Bilston, West Midlands WV14 7HZ
01902 404111

Wooden bathroom fittings; chrome, ceramic and antique gold finishes; bathroom suites and accessories

The Topstock Company

Higher Farm Barn, Milborne Wick, Sherborne, Dorset DT9 4PW
01963 250500

Light pulls, chain pulls and cistern levers. Mail order available.

Trevor Moore Handmade Designs

7 Weavers Walk, Northbrook Street, Newbury, Berkshire RG13 1AL
01380 727441

Customized fitted bathrooms. Hand-made washstands. Mail order available

---

Choosing Fittings

- Baths made of acrylic are the cheapest option, but they tend to scratch and mark easily, whereas pressed steel wears well and feels more solid. The most expensive option is cast iron, which is very hardwearing but also heavy – check that your floor is strong enough before you buy.
- White fittings are easy to keep clean and never date. Stronger colours show splashes and soap marks more easily and also limit your colour scheme when it comes to redecorating.
- Showers save water and energy. Most showers need a 'head' of at least five feet between the bottom of the water tank and the shower outlet. If you don't have this, you can install a power shower.
- Your WC is the biggest water user in your home. If you want to save water, choose a dual flush model

Beating the Steam

- Choose a paint that's suitable for bathrooms. Most manufacturers make special ranges that are resistant to damp, mould and humidity.
- Tiles are the safest choice in areas that get splashed with water. They'll need regular re-grouting and you may have to add more sealant to the join between tiles and fittings from time to time.
- If you have young children or the bathroom gets heavy wear and tear, vinyl or lino floors are the most practical option. If you choose carpet, check that it's suitable for bathrooms. Most wood floors can be damaged by damp and steam, so check with the manufacturer before you fit one.
- Good ventilation is essential – an extractor fan may help if you only have a small window and it's essential if the room doesn't have a window.

Free Planning Guide

The Bathroom Showroom Association has a free guide to planning and choosing a bathroom. Called The Essential Bathroom Guide, it's available by writing to Freepost ST3020, The Bathroom Showroom Association, Federation House, Stoke-on-Trent ST4 2BR.

3 • PAINTS

A fresh coat of paint is one of the easiest and cheapest ways to transform a room or update a piece of old furniture. There's been a colour revolution in the past few years and, as people have become more adventurous with the schemes they pick for their homes, so the choice of colours and finishes has increased. Now you can opt for traditional 'flat' oils and distempers in any number of authentic historical colours, or inject a burst of Mediterranean colour using brilliant powder or paste paints. The leading paint manufacturers have an excellent selection of colours in the traditional matt, eggshell and gloss finishes and there are plenty of smaller specialists who can offer you something a little different. And if you want to soften or strengthen the colour you've chosen, try your hand at paint effects.

Paints

Akzo Nobel Decorative Coating

PO Box 37, Hollins Road, Darwen, Lancashire BB3 0BG
Call 01254 704951 for advice and stockists

Sandtex paints and finishes for interior and exterior decorating

Annie Sloan

Relics, 35 Bridge Street, Witney, Oxfordshire OX8 6DA
01993 704611

Flat, matt, water-based paints in 24 colours. Particularly good for distempered, limewashed and distressed effects. Glazing medium available

AURO Organic Paint Supplies

Unit 1, Goldstones Farm, Ashdon, Saffron Walden, Essex
CB10 2LZ
01799 584 888

Around 50 traditional products including preservatives, stains, wood oil, waxes, varnishes and paints

B&Q

Call 0181 466 4166 for branches

Vinyl matt, silk and satin emulsions, kitchen and bathroom range and non-drip gloss. Water-based gloss and satinwood paints

Brats

281 King's Road, London SW3 5EW
0171 351 7674

Mediterranean Palette range of 27 colours including yellows, turquoises and pinks. Supplied in concentrate form to be diluted as required for a plaster, washed or matt finish

Brodie & Middleton

68 Drury Lane, London WC2B 5SP
0171 836 3289

Powder pigment in a range of colours. Ultraviolet pigment and liquid

Cole & Son (Wallpapers)

144 Offord Road, Islington, London N1 1NS
0171 607 4288

Oil-based eggshell, vinyl matt emulsion and wallpaper glaze

Craig & Rose

172 Leith Walk, Edinburgh EH6 5EB
0131 554 1131

A wide range of specialist decorating products, including distemper, lead paints and historic colours (including gold). Scumble glaze, varnishes, metallic paints and liquid stainers

Crown Paints

Call 01254 704 951 for stockist details

Extensive range in vinyl matt emulsion and vinyl silk. Also gloss, one-coat and cleanable paints, primer and undercoat. Mixed-to-order Expressions range

Do It All

Falcon House, The Minories, Dudley, West Midlands DY2 8PG
Call 0500 300 321 for local stores

Vinyl matt, silk and kitchen and bathroom emulsions in 36 colours, plus non-drip, liquid, one-coat and satin sheen gloss paints

Dulux

ICI Paints, Wexham Road, Slough, Berkshire SL2 5DS
01753 550555

Matt emulsion, silk, satinwood and gloss paints. Also water-based gloss for wood, metal and outdoor paints. Range of 250 Heritage Colours from Dulux Trade, based on authentic colours from Georgian, Victorian, Edwardian and Art Deco eras

Farrow & Ball

249 Fulham Road, London SW3 3HY
0171 351 0273

National Trust range of 57 paints based on colours used in historic properties. Archive range with a further 38 historic colours. Seven paint types, including flat oils and distempers. Available by mail order. Bespoke colour-matching service also available

Fired Earth

Twyford Mill, Oxford Road, Adderbury, Oxon OX17 3HP
01295 814300 for brochures and stockists

A range of 18 historic colours developed in conjunction with the V & A. Range includes flat oil and distemper, as well as emulsion, eggshell and semi-matt gloss. Mail order available

Foxell & James

57 Farringdon Road, London EC1M 3JB
0171 405 0152

Own-brand traditional paints. Wide range of specialist products, including metallic and marbling paints, scumble glaze, distemper, varnish and gilding materials. Stencils

Hammerite

Prudhoe, Northumberland NE42 6LP
01661 830000

Metal paint in 26 colour and finish combinations for indoor and outdoor use

Heart of the Country

Home Farm, Swinfen, Nr Lichfield, Staffordshire, WS14 9QR
01543 481612

Period colours from Victorian, federal and colonial eras made from natural earth pigments. Oil base, low sheen, velvet finish with the economy of normal one-coat coverage. Range of Buttermilk Paints with matt finish

Homestyle

Victoria Mills, Macclesfield Road, Holmes Chapel, Crewe, Cheshire CW4 7PA
Call 0990 133610 for local stores

Matt and silk emulsion, satin and new soft sheen emulsion, non-drip, liquid and one-coat gloss. Also kitchen and bathroom paints, outdoor paints, wood stains and varnishes

Jane Churchill

249 Fulham Road, London SW3
01202 876141 (Farrow & Ball)

Thirty-nine paint colours available in matt emulsion, eggshell, undercoat and gloss by mail order with delivery within five working days

John Oliver

33 Pembridge Road, London W11 3HG
0171 221 6466

Exclusive range of paints in 40 colours. Authentic shades from The Historical Book of Colours. Floor paint in a wide range of colours to order. Paint-mixing service. Mail order available

Johnstone's
(Kalon Decorative Products)

Huddersfield Road, Birstall, Batley, West Yorkshire WF17 9XA
01924 477201

Vinyl matt emulsion, silk and gloss paints. Also outdoor paints, floor paints and timber preservative in a range of colours

J W Bollom

15 Theobalds Road, London WC1X 8SN
0171 242 0313

Own-brand premium quality paints in all finishes. Flame-retardant paints. Specialist varnishes and equipment for paint effects

L Cornelisson & Son

105 Great Russell Street, London WC1B 3RY
0171 636 1045

Materials for paint and gilding effects. Mail order available

Leyland

Call 01924 420202 for nearest stockist

Complete range of decorative paints and wood finishes, including vinyl matt, silk and soft sheen, non-drip and traditional liquid gloss. Ready-mixed colours and Complements System, which offers over 5,000 shades

Nutshell Natural Paints

Hamlyn House, Buckfastleigh, Devon TQ11 0NR
01364 642892

Casein Milk Paint (distemper) that is mixed up with Earth and Mineral pigments. Mail order available

Omnihome

77 Golborne Road, London W10 5NP
0181 964 2100

Mediterranean-inspired range of vinyl-free paints in 14 colours. Sold in economical paste formula to be used neat or thinned to create washed, sponged and distressed finishes. Ultra matt finish

Paint Library

5 Elystan Street, London SW3 3NT
0171 823 7755

Hand-mixed paint in a range of colours and finishes. Also glazes, metallic paints, colour matching and 'interference paint' which creates a two-tone effect similar to shot silk

Paint Magic Jocasta Innes

79 Shepperton Road, London N1 3DF
0171 354 9696 (mail order 0171 226 4420)

Range of 12 matt colours, plus ready-tinted distempers in five shades. Limewash, woodwash, colour wash, pure pigments, stencils and stamps, gilding and verdigris kits

Papers and Paints

4 Park Walk, London SW10 0AD
0171 352 8626

Exclusive traditional, historical and off-white paint ranges. Shop also stocks Sanderson paints, varnishes, glazes, brushes, tools, pigments and paint-effects books

Plascon International

Retail Division, 24–30 Canute Road, Southampton SO14 3PB
01703 226722

Outdoor paints and wood stains, primers and undercoats. Floor and radiator paints, floor varnish, Japlac high gloss lacquer, anti-condensation and anti-stain formulas, anti-burglar and child-safe paints. Garage floor paint and anti-mould and damp formulas

Plasti-Kote

London Road Industrial Estate, Sawston, Cambridge CB2 4TR
01223 836400

Water-, enamel-, and acrylic-based spray paints for wood, plastic, enamel and walls. Also paints for kitchen appliances, wood stoves and vinyl. Anti-rust formulas. Stain-Stop for water stains and ceiling marks

Portmolen Paints

27 Woodcock Industrial Estate, Warminster, Wiltshire
BA12 9DX
01985 213960

Traditional distempers, lead and linseed-oil paints. Limewashes and wax and oil recipes

Sanderson

112–120 Brompton Road, London SW3 1JJ
Call 0171 584 3344 for stockist information

Extensive Spectrum paint range in gloss, eggshell, vinyl matt emulsion and vinyl silk emulsion

Shaker

322 King's Road, London SW3 5UH
Call 0171 724 7672 for mail order

Wood paints in a range of eight traditional Shaker colours

Wickes Building Supplies

Wickes House, 120–138 Station Road, Harrow, Middlesex
HA1 2QB
Call 0500 300 328 for your nearest store

Master range of matt and silk emulsion, gloss, satin-coat and non-drip gloss. Also one-coat, low-odour, kitchen, bathroom and masonry paints. Water-based quick drying gloss in white only. Exterior gloss

---

Colour Matching

If you want to match paint to a fabric or repaint your walls in exactly the same shade but you can't find the right colour anywhere, try a bespoke colour-matching service. Several companies, among them Farrow & Ball and Paint Library (see addresses) offer this. Or you could try the Dulux Spectrophotometer available at selected branches of John Lewis. Take a fabric or paint sample along and the special machine will recreate the colour 'recipe'. This shade can then be mixed by a machine in the store. For more information, contact your local branch of John Lewis or ring head office on 0171 828 1000.

Wood Stains and Finishes

Akzo Nobel Woodcare

Sadolin House, Meadow Lane, St Ives, Cambridgeshire
PE17 4UY
01480 496868

Range of decorative wood protection products for exterior and interior use

Cuprinol

Adderwell, Frome, Somerset BA11 1NL
01373 465151

Wood stains for interior and exterior use. Also wood treatments and varnishes, anti-damp treatments and wood preservatives

Liberon Waxes

Mountfield Industrial Estate, Learoyd Road, New Romney, Kent TN28 8XU
01797 367555

Wood dyes, waxes, fillers and sealers. Also 'reviver' for marble, terracotta, stone and slate. French polishes

Os Color

Ostermann & Scheiwe UK Ltd, Ickenham, Middx UB10 8QD
01895 252171

Natural oil-based wood finishes for interior and exterior use. Available in semi-transparent, satin matte, opaque semi-gloss, pastels, country colours, clear and wood finish. Preservatives and wood wax finishes

Ronseal

Stornclife Park, Chapeltown, Sheffield S30 4YP
01142 467171

Extensive floor and furniture care range, including fillers, wax, oil and waterproof wood stain. Wood colouring for floors and furniture

Stencil Suppliers

Angela Beaumont

12–14 Hainworth Village, Keighley, West Yorkshire BD21 5QH
01535 604381

Period stencil specialist. Designs to commission

L G Harris & Co

Stoke Prior, Bromsgrove, Worcestershire B60 4AE
01527 575441

Traditional and nursery stencils, paint, stamps and accessories. Mail order available

The Painted Finish

Unit 6, Hatton Country World, Hatton, Warwick CV35 8XA
01926 842376

Large range of stencils, paints and accessories. Scumbles, glazes and crackles, fabric and ceramic paints. Range of MDF products for painting and decorating

The Stencil Factory

105 Upgate, Louth, Lincolnshire LN11 9HF
01507 600948

Large range of stencils and designs to commission. Accessories and mail order available

The Stencil Library

Nesbitt Hill Head, Stamfordham, Northumberland NE18 0LG
01661 844844

Around 1,000 different designs. Paints and accessories available. Workshops on stencilling, decoupage and paint effects. Design to commission. Mail order

The Stencil Store

20–21 Heronsgate Road, Chorleywood, Hertfordshire
WD3 5BN
01923 285577 for nearest store and mail order

Stencil equipment, tools for paint effects, paints, ceramic paints, ageing and antiquing kits. Stencilling workshops

Creating Paint Effects

Paint effects are one of the quickest and easiest ways to transform walls and furniture and you can use them to create antique effects or soften harsh colours. They're also excellent for covering uneven or imperfect walls. Try out the effect of different colours on a piece of card or wood before you start.

- Colour Washing
  Depth and intensity are added to a colour scheme by applying several weak layers of wash (thinned water-based paint) or glaze (thinned oil-based paint) over a base colour. The overall effect is very warm and easy on the eye.

- Sponging
  This is a technique for adding soft spots of colour using a sponge. It's one of the easiest effects to create, all you need is a natural sponge (man-made versions create too uniform an effect). You can either sponge on (add colour to a layer of matt paint) or sponge off (use a sponge to remove colour). Similar effects can be created using a rag (ragging) or brush (stippling).

- Dragging
  A striped, grainy effect is achieved by pulling a dry brush through wet glaze. It works on walls or woodwork and you can create similar grained textures using a comb (combing) or wood-graining tool.

4 • FABRICS AND WALLCOVERINGS

You can use fabric and wallcoverings to create just about any style you want, from the classic English country-house look, to bold eastern and ethnic effects. Co-ordinated fabric and wallpaper collections take the stress out of choosing papers, borders and fabrics that match and make it easy to produce a decorating scheme that works. And if you're looking for something specific – whether it's an authentic period wallpaper or a Provençal print – we've listed companies that can help.

Co-ordinated Collections

Fabric and wallcoverings for a classic co-ordinated look:

Andrew Martin

200 Walton Street, London SW3 2JL
0171 584 4290

Anna French

343 King's Road, London SW3 5ES
0171 351 1126

Ashley Wilde

Gilbey Textiles Ltd, Giltex House, Cline Road, London N11 2LR
0181 368 6860

Colefax & Fowler

39 Brook Street, London W1Y 2JE
0171 493 2231

Coloroll

John Wilman Ltd, Riverside Mills, Crawford Street, Nelson,
Lancashire BB9 7QT
01282 617777

Crown Wallcoverings

Call 01254 704213 for stockists

Crowson Fabrics

Crowson House, Bellbrook Park, Uckfield, East Sussex
TN22 1QZ
01825 761055

Decorative Fabrics Gallery

278–280 Brompton Road, London SW3 2AS
0171 589 4778

Forbo Lancaster

Lune Mills, Lancaster LA1 5QN
01524 65222

Harlequin Fabrics & Wallcoverings

Cossington Road, Sileby, Leicestershire LE12 7RU
01509 816575

Homestyle

Call 01477 544544 for stockists

Jane Churchill

151 Sloane Street, London SW1X 9BX
0181 874 6484

John Wilman

Call 0800 581984 for stockists

K A International

68 Sloane Avenue, London SW3 3DD
0171 584 7352

Laura Ashley

150 Bath Road, Maidenhead, Berkshire SL6 4XS
01686 622116

Linda Beard Textile Division

Giltex House, Clive Road, London N11 2LR
0181 368 9566

Marks & Spencer

Michael House, 47 Baker Street, London W1A 1DN
0171 935 4422

Marvic Textiles

Unit 1, Westpoint Trading Estate, Alliance Road, Acton, London W3 0RA
0181 993 0191

Montgomery Interior Fabrics

Call 01244 661363 for stockists

Next Interiors

Call 0345 100500 for orders and inquiries

Nina Campbell

9 Walton Street, London SW3 2JD
0171 225 1011

Nono Designs

98 Bridge Street, Macclesfield, Cheshire SK11 6QA
01625 500405

Osborne & Little

304 King's Road, London SW3 5UH
0171 352 1456

Paper Moon

53 Fairfax Road, London NW6 4EL
0171 624 1198

Parker Knoll Fabrics & Wallpapers (Parkertex)

Call 01494 467400 for stockists

Romo Fabrics

Lowmoor Road, Kirkby in Ashfield, Nottinghamshire NG17 7DE
01623 750005

Sandberg

Call 0800 967222 for local stockists

Sanderson

112–120 Brompton Road, London SW3 1JJ
0171 584 3344

Streets Interior Textiles

Call 01268 766677 for local stockists

Vymura

Call 0161 368 8321 for local stockists

Warner Fabrics

Bradbourne Drive, Tilbrook, Milton Keynes MK7 8BE
01908 366900

Whiteheads Fabrics

Dominion Way West, Southdownview Road, Worthing, West Sussex BN14 8NT
01903 212222

Fabric Specialists

Anta Scotland

Call 01862 832477 for a catalogue

Wool and silk tartans and tweeds

Borderline

Unit 7, Second Floor, Chelsea Harbour Design Centre, London SW10 0XE
0171 823 3567

Archive design cotton, wool and silk. Trimmings

Chelsea Textiles

7 Walton Street, London SW3 2JD
0171 584 0111

Crewelwork fabrics

Ciel Decor

187 New King's Road, London SW6 4SW
0171 731 0444

Provençal prints

Designers Guild

277 King's Road, London SW3 5EN
0171 351 5775

Fabrics and wallcoverings in bright, contemporary colours and designs

Habitat

196 Tottenham Court Road, London W1P 9LD
0645 334433 for local branches

Contemporary fabrics and ready-made curtains and blinds

Ian Mankin

109 Regent's Park Road, London NW1 8UR
0171 722 0997

Cottons and sheer fabrics in checks, stripes and weaves

Ikea

2 Drury Way, North Circular Road, London NW10 0TH
0181 208 5600

Good-value furnishing fabrics in contemporary designs

Jab Anstoetz

Call 0171 349 9323 for stockists

Large range of distinctive printed and woven fabrics

Java Cotton

3 Blenheim Crescent, London W11 2EE
0171 229 3212

Cotton batiks

John Lewis

278–306 Oxford Street, London W1A 1EX
0171 629 7711

Large range of curtain and upholstery fabric under Jonelle brand. Also stocks wide selection of other brands. Efficient curtain make-up and upholstery service

Liberty

Regent Street, London W1R 6AH
0171 734 1234

Wide range of fabrics, including Liberty prints

Malabar

31–33 Southbank Business Centre, Ponton Road, London SW8 5BL
0171 501 4200

Bold cotton Madras checks, stripes and plains

Natural Fabric Company

Wessex Place, Hungerford, Berkshire RG17 0DL
01488 684002

Gingham, damask and Irish linen

Pukka Palace

The Market Hall, Craven Arms, Shropshire SY7 9NZ
01588 672999

Ethnic fabrics

Russell & Chapple

23 Monmouth Street, London WC2H 9DE
0171 836 7521

Canvas and cotton

Timney-Fowler

388 King's Road, London SW3 5UZ
0171 352 2263

Distinctive black and white fabrics taken from classical designs

Wolfin

64 Great Titchfield Street, London W1P 7AE
0171 636 4949

Linings and interlinings

Easy Sewing

Soft furnishings can be made very simply if you cheat and use kits and sewing aids. Staple guns (available from tool-hire shops) can be used to create instant fabric panels or fix new seat covers on dining chairs. And look out for iron-on hem and pelmet kits. If you want the ultimate fix for a cushion, seat or duvet cover, try Velcro instead of buttons.

- Harrison Drape
  Call 0121 766 6111 for stockists
  Curtain clips

- Speedy Products
  Call 0161 737 1001 for stockists
  Produces 'no-sew' eyelet kits for simple buttonholes or curtain headings

- Vilene
  PO Box 3, Ellistones Lane, Halifax, West Yorkshire HX4 8NJ
  01422 313140
  Makes pelmet kits, Bondahem iron-on hem kits

Fabric Facts

- Sofas and chairs should always be covered in upholstery-strength weaves. Look for Scotchgard-treated fabrics, or ask your upholsterer to treat the fabric for you. (Scotchgard fabric protector Helpline 0800 581546.)
- Curtains need to hang properly, so make sure the material isn't too stiff. A lining can be used to add weight to lighter fabrics. Make sure you choose a fabric that will block out the light if the curtains are for a bedroom.
- Buy all the fabric you need in one batch as variations may occur in dyeing or printing.
- If you're making your own lined curtains or soft furnishings, make sure the lining, trim and fabric are compatible when it comes to washing or dry cleaning.
- If you have young children, look for durable, washable materials.

Soft Furnishings by Post

Designer Fabrics 01270 610032
Fabrics & Wallpaper 01376 517800
Fabrics & Wallpaper Direct 01782 628987
Fabrics Unlimited 01372 454532
Home Interiors 0800 387473

Wallcoverings Specialists

Alexander Beauchamp

Griffin Mill, Thrupp, Stroud, Gloucestershire GL5 2AZ
01453 884537

Period paper. Any colourway to order

Baer & Ingram Wallpapers

273 Wandsworth Bridge Road, London SW6 2TX
0171 736 6111

Traditional hand-printed papers in damask and moire, plus stripes and florals. Also stocks own range of fabrics

Cole & Son

142–144 Oxford Road, London N1 1NS
0171 607 4288

Hand-printed and screen-printed wallpapers

Hamilton Weston

18 St Mary's Grove, Richmond, Surrey TW9 1UY
0181 940 4850

Copies of authentic period papers. Can reproduce designs

John Oliver

33 Pembridge Road, London W11 3HG
0171 221 6466

Own range of distinctive hand- and machine-printed wallpapers. Any colourway to order. Specialist in metallics and marbled papers

Stick-on Effects

Transform a plain wall using stick-on borders, columns, swags and other embellishments. The following companies offer good selections, but for an inexpensive DIY version, photocopy an old engraving, print or architectural drawing and stick it on the wall using border adhesive (try the Dover Street Book Shop, 18 Earlham Street, London WC2H, 0171 836 2111 for an excellent range of source books). A coat of clear varnish over the top will protect the design.

- Arc
  103 Wandsworth Bridge Road, London SW6 2TE
  0171 731 3933

- John Sutcliffe
  PO Box 142, Cambridge CB3 0SG
  Write for brochure

- National Trust
  Blewcoat School Gift Shop, 23 Caxton Street, London SW1 0PY
  0171 222 2877

5 • TILES

Tiles are a practical way to avoid splashes and water damage, but they can also introduce colour and pattern to functional areas like kitchens, bathrooms and utility rooms. The choice is vast, with Mediterranean, Mexican and vivid glazed plains becoming increasingly popular. You can customize the look, by mixing colours or adding detailing with patterned tiles or borders. If you are stuck with tiles in a colour or style you don't like, or would like to introduce a pattern without the expense of re-tiling, there are excellent tile paints and stick-on motifs available.

Candy & Co

Great Western Potteries, Heathfield, Newton Abbot, Devon
TQ12 6RF
01626 832641

Victorian-style ceramic tiles. Plain tiles and borders in a range of colours

Carol Sinclair Ceramics

Unit 3, Albion Business Centre, 78 Albion Road, Edinburgh
EH7 5QZ
0131 652 0490

Hand-made and hand-painted ceramic tiles in contemporary and traditional designs

Criterion Tiles

196 Wandsworth Bridge Rd, London SW6 2UF
0171 736 9610

English and continental hand-decorated and hand-made tiles

Decorum Ceramic Studio

Norths Estate, Piddington, Bucks HP14 3BE
01494 882299

Hand-painted ceramic tiles for bathrooms and kitchens

Fired Earth

Twyford Mill, Oxford Road, Aderbury, Oxon OX17 3HP
01295 812088

Wide range of terracotta and ceramic tiles and borders in various colours and finishes. Also Roman-style mosaic tiles

H & R Johnson

Highgate Tile Works, Brownhills Road, Tunstall, Staffordshire ST6 4JX
01782 575575

Extensive range of decorated tiles

Julie Arnall

26 Woodwaye, Watford, Herts WD1 4NW
01923 228465

Hand-painted original designs, glazed and patterned tiles including signs of the zodiac, Roman numerals and English wildlife

Kenneth Clark Ceramics

The North Wing, Southover Grange, Southover Road, Lewes, East Sussex BN7 1TP
01273 476761

Made to order hand-decorated glazed ceramic tiles in geometrics, figurative and floral designs. Also relief finishes and hand-stencilled and hand-painted ranges

Marlborough Fine English Tiles

Elcot Lane, Marlborough SN8 2AY
01672 512422

Ceramic tiles in a wide range of designs

Metropolitan Tile Co

Lower Audley Centre, Kent Street, Blackburn, Lancs BB1 1DE
01254 695111

Hand-made wall tiles in rustic designs. Fabric matching available

Original Style

Falcon Road, Exeter EX2 7LF
01392 474059

Wide range of ceramic wall tiles

Philip & Tacey

North Way, Andover, Hants SP10 5BA
01264 332171

Hand-painted tiles in terracotta, ceramic and glazed finishes

Pilkington's Tiles

PO Box 4, Clifton Junction, Manchester M27 8LP
0161 727 1001

Hand-painted ceramic and dust-pressed tiles for kitchens and bathrooms

Reject Tile Shop

178 Wandsworth Bridge Road, London SW6 2UQ
0171 731 6098

Large stock of seconds and end-of-line tiles. Some imported hand- and machine-made tiles

Reptile

Gwaith Menyn, Llanglydwen, Whitland, Carmarthenshire
SA34 0XP
01994 419402

Ceramic hand-painted tiles in sea life, nautical and flower designs

Rye Tiles

The Old Brewery, Wishward, Rye, Sussex TN31 7DH
01797 223038
12 Connaught Street, London W2 2AF
0171 723 7278

Screen-printed and hand-painted ceramic tiles and murals made to order

Sally Anderson (Ceramics)

Parndon Mill, Harlow CM20 2HP
01279 420982

Hand-decorated ceramic tiles and murals. Modern, traditional and classical designs

The Life Enhancing Tile Company

Alliance House, 14–28 St Mary's Road, Portsmouth, Hants
PO1 5PH
0117 907 7673

Hand-made ceramic tiles. Specialists in decorative encaustic finishes and unglazed ceramic tiles with inlaid decoration

The Tile Gallery

1 Royal Parade, 247 Dawes Road, London SW6 7RE
0171 385 8818

Ceramic, encaustic, marble and terracotta tiles. Hand-painted and hand-glazed ranges

The Winchester Tile Co

Unit C1, Pegasus Court, Ardglen Road, Whitchurch RG28 7BP
01256 896922

Hand-made ceramic wall tiles in a range of original designs

Tiles of Stow

Langston Priory Workshops, Station Road, Kingham OX7 6UP
01608 658993

Hand-decorated wall tiles in a range of original designs

Wellington Tile Co

Milverton Road, Wellington TA21 0AZ
01823 667242

Hand-made French glazed-terracotta tiles

And If You Can't Re-tile . . .

From special paints, to stick-on ceramic motifs, the following companies offer products to help you revamp old tiles:

- Crystal Palace Pottery
  PO Box 4259, London SE26 6TG
  0181 761 9490
  Decorative ceramic motifs for transforming plain tiles
- Pebeo UK
  PO Box 556, Southampton SO16 7ZF
  Call 01703 901914 for stockists
  Porcelain paints for creating your own designs on ceramics
- Plascon International
  Retail Division, 24–30 Canute Road, Southampton, Hampshire
  SO14 3PB
  01703 226722
  Special ceramic paints

- Sticky Solutions
  PO Box 5, Beverley, East Yorkshire HU17 8YZ
  01482 784379
  Adhesive stick-on designs for tiles

- The English Stamp Co
  Worth Matravers, Dorset BH19 3JP
  01929 439117
  Motifs and decorative stamps for transforming plain tiles

6 • FURNITURE

Nothing sets the tone of your home as quickly as furniture – which is why it can be so difficult to choose. Before you go shopping, take careful measurements of the room you're buying for (remember to check the measurements of doorways and staircases, too). You also need to assess the amount of light it receives – large or dark pieces of furniture may overpower darker or smaller areas and make them feel cluttered. If space is restricted, look for pieces that have a dual role – for example, tables with storage cupboards or shelves underneath. Flatpack furniture and divan beds can ease the squeeze if access is really restricted. And before you invest in large items like wardrobes, cupboards and dressers, it's worth remembering that the most useful pieces are those that can be adapted or will slot in somewhere else if you change the layout of a room or move house.

Traditional Designs

Brights of Nettlebed

Kingston House, Nettlebed, Henley-on-Thames, Oxfordshire
RG9 5DD
01491 641115

Warehouse full of reproduction furniture. Tailor-made upholstery

British Antique Replicas

School Close, Queen Elizabeth Avenue, Burgess Hill, West Sussex RH15 9RX
01444 245577

Reproduction tables, chairs, sideboards, desks, filing, cocktail and TV cabinets. Also leather chairs and Chesterfields

Ducal

Andover, Hampshire SP10 5AZ
01264 333666

Complete range of traditional wooden designs, including dining tables, chairs, sideboards and bedroom furniture

Ercol

Freepost, Slough SL1 4BU
For a catalogue, call 01753 536600

Extensive range of wood-framed sofas and chairs, plus tables and occasional furniture

Grand Illusions

2–4 Crown Road, St Margarets, Twickenham TW1 3EE
0181 744 1046

Sophisticated country-style designs painted to order. Excellent range of traditional home office furniture

Jaycee

Bexhill Road, Brighton BN2 6QQ
01273 304081

Traditional and reproduction dining and occasional furniture

J Sydney Smith

The Tannery, Leeds Road, Otley LS21 1QX
01943 462321

Mahogany and yew period furniture

Lancashire Reproductions

Call 0800 137621 for a brochure

Traditional desks and leather office chairs

Laura Ashley

Call 01686 622116 for stockists

Wide range of furniture, including sofas and occasional pieces

Maples Stores

Call 01926 404000 for local stores

Extensive range of dining-room and sitting-room furniture

Marks & Spencer

Michael House, Baker Street, London W1A 1DN
0171 935 4422

Traditional styles in pine and dark wood, plus sofas, chairs and beds

Maun Valley Woodworking

Leeming Lane South, Mansfield Woodehouse, Nottinghamshire
NG19 9AQ
01623 636393

Oak furniture, including corner units, cabinets and tables

Nathan Furniture

Angel Road, London N18 3AD
0181 803 4241

Traditional wooden furniture, including hi-fi cabinets and tables

Peter Guild

84–92 College Street, Kempston, Bedford MK42 8LU
01234 273372

Traditional footstools and furniture, including three-piece suites

Pine Mine

100 Wandsworth Bridge Road, London SW6 2TF
0171 736 1092

Large stock of old and new pine furniture

Richard Kimbell

Rockingham Road, Market Harborough, Leicestershire
LE16 7QE
01858 433444

Country-style furniture. Range includes an ingenious foldaway home office

Sanderson

112–120 Brompton Road, London SW3 1JJ
0171 584 3344

Sofas and chairs covered in Sanderson fabrics

Stag Furniture

Park Drive, Hucknall, Nottinghamshire NG15 7LU
0115 9634314

Extensive range of traditional dining, occasional and bedroom furniture

Strongbow

William Bartlett & Son, PO Box 42, Sheraton Works, Grafton Street, High Wycombe, Buckinghamshire HP12 3AL
01494 526491

Traditional designs in mahogany and yew

Westminster Pine

Unit 3, Abenbury Way Industrial Estate, Wrexham, Clwyd
LL13 9UZ
01978 661300

Traditional telephone tables and hall seats

Wood Bros

London Road, Ware, Hertfordshire SG12 9QH
01920 469241

Traditional and reproduction dining and occasional furniture

Contemporary Looks

Aero

96 Westbourne Grove, London W2 5RT
0171 221 1950

Sleek modern furniture and accessories

Beaver & Tapley

Call 0181 574 4311 for a catalogue

Freestanding and fitted furniture

Cane Connection

57 Wimbledon Hill Road, London SW19 7QW
0181 947 9152

Cane tables, chairs and occasional furniture

Conran Shop

Michelin House, 81 Fulham Road, London SW3 6RD
0171 589 7401

Impressive collection of contemporary furniture and accessories

CubeStore

38 Grosvenor Road, London W4 4EG
0181 994 6016

Low-cost storage units and wardrobes

Designers Guild

277 King's Road, London SW3 5EN
0171 351 5775

Contemporary furniture and accessories

Habitat

Call 0645 334433 for local stores

Classic modern furniture: tables, chairs, sofas, beds and wardrobes

Heal's

196 Tottenham Court Road, London W1P 9LD
0171 636 1666

Well-made contemporary furniture and accessories

Holding Company

243–245 King's Road, London SW3 5EL
0171 610 9160

Clever storage ideas, including home office and bedroom furniture and accessories

Homebase

Call 0645 801800 for stores

Good range of storage ideas

Ikea

2 Drury Way, North Circular Road, London NW10 0TH
0181 208 5600

Complete range of budget furniture, including chairs, tables, sofas and beds and storage units. Large selection of flatpack designs. Also stocks distinctive Swedish designer pieces

Iron Design Company

Summer Carr Farm, Thornton Le Moor, Northallerton, North Yorkshire DL6 3SG
01609 778143

Hand-made iron furniture influenced by Italianate, gothic and rococo designs. Also makes to commission

Ligne Roset

95a High Street, Great Missenden, Buckinghamshire HP16 0AL
01494 865001

Modern furniture

MFI Home Works

Call 0500 192192 for your local store

Functional designs at good value prices. Large selection of flatpack furniture. Also fitted furniture

Ocean Home Shopping

Freepost LON811, London SW8 4BR
0800 132 985

Stylish contemporary furniture and accessories

Purves & Purves

80–81 & 83 Tottenham Court Road, London W1P 9HD
0171 580 8223 (01709 889900 to request catalogue)

Distinctive modern furniture and accessories

Shaker

322 King's Road, London SW3 5UH
0171 352 3918

Shaker-influenced furniture and accessories

The Pier

200 Tottenham Court Road, London W1 0AD
0171 814 5020

Ethnic and contemporary pine, dark wood and rattan furniture, rugs and accessories

The Source

Unit B3, Lakeside Retail Park, West Thurrock RM16 1WS
01708 890253
26–40 Kensington High Street, London W8 4PF
0171 937 2626

One-stop shop for contemporary furniture and soft furnishings. Competitive prices

Wharfside Danish Furniture

66 Buttesland Street, London N1 6BY
0171 253 3206

Dining-room, living-room and office furniture from Scandinavia

Sofa Specialists

A Barn Full of Sofas and Chairs

Furnace Mill, Lamberhurst, Kent TN3 8LH
01892 890285

Antique, period and secondhand furniture. Buy as seen or have it re-upholstered in your choice of fabric. Open Tuesday to Saturday

Classic Choice

Call 01656 721006 for a brochure

Sofas and three-piece suites by mail order

Highly Sprung

85–89 Chiswick High Road, London W14 9EF
0181 742 7943

Large range of sofas, sofabeds and chairs

Kingdom of Leather

Unit 3, Gallions Road, London SE7 7SA
0181 305 0101

Large selection of leather sofas and chairs

Kirkdale Mail Order

Viaduct Works, Crumlin Road, Crumlin, Gwent NP1 4PL
01495 243999

Sofas and chairs by mail order

Parker Knoll

The Courtyard, Frogmoor, High Wycombe, Buckinghamshire
HP13 5DD
01494 521144

Chairs, sofas and sofabeds

Scandecor

20 Castle Street, Brighton BN1 2HD
01273 820208

Victorian- and Edwardian-style chesterfields, wing chairs and chaises-longues in leather or fabric. Also Art Deco and 1920s designs

Sofa Workshop Direct

Coedcae Lane, Pontyclun, S Wales CF72 9DX
01443 238699

Sofas and chairs by mail order

The Sofabed Factory

258–260 Lavender Hill, London SW11 1LJ
0171 228 4588

Sofabed specialists

Thomas Lloyd

Unit 11, Abergorki Industrial Estate, Treorchy, Mid Glamorgan
CF42 6DL
01443 771333

Leather sofas and chairs in traditional and contemporary designs

Tulleys of Chelsea

289–297 Fulham Road, London SW10 9PZ
0171 352 1078

Classic sofas and chairs made in the company's own workshop. Also stocks beds

World of Leather

Jubilee Square, London Road, Reading, Berkshire RG1 2TA
01734 861481

Massive selection of leather sofas and chairs

Beds and Bedsteads

Billie Bond

2 Warners Farm Cottage, Howe Street, Great Waltham,
Chelmsford, Essex CM3 1BL
01245 360164

Traditional bedsteads and bedroom and nursery furniture

Brass Knight

Cumeragh House Farm, Cumeragh Lane, Whittingham, Preston, Lancashire PR3 2AL
01772 786666

Original Victorian beds

British Waterbed Company

228 Withycombe Village Road, Exmouth, Devon EX8 3BD
01395 268866

Waterbed specialists

Deptich Designs

7 College Fields, Prince George's Road, London SW19 2PT
0181 687 0867

Lits bateaux

Dreams Bed Superstores

Call 01628 535353 for your nearest store

Bed superstores with wide range of prices

Gainsborough

Ladydown Estate, Trowbridge, Wiltshire BA14 8RL
01225 766341

Zip and link beds

Hoppe Designs

Call 01432 851590

Makes a compact foldaway design called 'bed in a box'

Layeezee Beds

Soothill Lane, Batley, West Yorkshire WF17 6LJ
01924 441818

Sprung-slatted beds

Mitre Pine Beds

The Old Stable, Bishop Road, Bishopston, Bristol
0117 9496449

Pine and hardwood beds. Waxed and colour-washed finishes available. Made-to-measure service

Moriarti's Workshop

Call 01233 850214 for a brochure

Wooden and storage beds

Morpheus

1 New Church Street, Tetbury, Gloucestershire GL8 8DS
01666 504068

Traditional beds, including lits bateaux

Once Upon a Time

The Green Ripley, Surrey GU23 6AL
01483 211330

Antique beds

Reylon

Staion Mills, PO Box 1, Wellington, Somerset TA21 8NN
01823 667501

Beds made to order in special sizes

Seventh Heaven

Chirk Mill, Chirk, Wrexham LL14 5BU
01691 777622

Antique beds, plus mattresses, bedroom furniture and traditional bedlinen

S W Antiques

Abbey Showrooms, Newlands, Pershore, Worcestershire WR10 1BP
01386 555580

Period beds and matching furniture

The Antique Brass Bedstead Company

Baddow Antique Centre, Great Baddow, Chelmsford, Essex CM2 7JW
01245 471137

Large range of Victorian iron and brass bedsteads

The Futon Company

138 Notting Hill Gate, London W11 3QG
0171 727 9252

Futons and four posters

Neat Solutions

If space is at a premium, or you want to create a bedroom-cum-office, fitted bedroom furniture is a good option. The following companies specialize in tailoring storage space to suit small areas:

- Christies
  Call 0800 446655 for a brochure
- Hammonds Furniture
  Call 01455 251505 for a brochure

- Hulsta
  Call 0171 629 4881 for a brochure

- Neville Johnson Offices
  Call 0161 873 8333

- Sharps Bedrooms
  Call 0800 789789 for your nearest showroom

- Spacemaker
  Call 01277 229223 for a brochure

- The London Wall Bed Company
  Call 0181 742 8200

Bright Ideas

One cost-effective solution is to transform simple MDF furniture with paint or fabric. Many DIY stores stock tables, or you can have MDF cut to size for simple shelves and tables. The following specialists make everything from headboards to wardrobes:

- Harvey Baker
  Call 01803 521515
  Excellent range of MDF pieces

- Scumble Goosie
  01453 731305

- The Dormy House
  Call 01264 365789 for a brochure
  MDF TV and video tables, dressing tables, headboards, footstools, chairs, filing ottomans and screens

- Till Joinery
  Call 01737 361294 for a brochure
  Radiator covers, wardrobes, bookcases and kitchen units. Also MDF furniture made to order

---

7 • FLOORING

There's a vast choice of floorings – from ceramic tiles to intricately patterned Axminster carpets. The biggest trend in recent years has been towards natural floor coverings in coir, sisal, seagrass and jute. Indeed they've become so popular that carpet manufacturers have begun creating natural effects with traditional wool. Tiles in vinyl or cork are still the most practical option for kitchens and bathrooms and there's a huge choice of colours and patterns. For a more natural look, opt for wood or laminate in strips, boards and parquet, or use traditional flagstones to create a classic country style.

Carpets and Natural Floorcoverings

Afia Carpets of London

Chelsea Harbour Design Centre, London SW10 0XE
0171 351 5858

Wool and man-made carpets in patterns and plains. Dye-to-order service. Fitting available

Allied Carpets

Call 01689 895000 for stockists and information

Wool and man-made carpets in patterns and plains. Made-to-order Ryalux carpets. Fitting available

Axminster Carpets

Axminster, Devon EX13 5PQ
01297 32244

British wool carpets in patterns, tonals and borders. Fitting through retailers

BMK

Kilmarnock KA1 1SX
01563 578000

Wool-based patterns and plains. Fitting through retailers

Brintons

PO Box 16, Exchange Street, Kidderminster, Worcestershire DY10 1AG
01562 820000

Wool-based patterns and plains. Fitting through retailers

Brockway Carpets

Kidderminster Trading Estate, Spennels Valley Road, Kidderminster, Worcester DY10 1XS
01562 747877

Wool-based and man-made plain and tufted carpets. Fitting through retailers

Carpets International UK

Toftshaw Lane, Bradford BD4 6QW
01274 681881

Wool and man-made plain carpets, including Wilton styles. Fitting through retailers

Cormar Carpets

Brookhouse Mill, Greenmount, Bury, Lancashire BL8 4HR
01204 882241

Wool and man-made plain and tufted carpets. Fitting through retailers

Crucial Trading

79 Westbourne Park Road, London W2
0171 221 9000

Large range of natural floor coverings, including coloured and patterned designs

Fired Earth

Twyford Mill, Oxford Road, Adderbury, Oxfordshire
OX17 3HP
01295 812088

Natural floor coverings in plain and patterned weaves. Fitting available

Firth Carpets

PO Box 17, Clifton Mills, Brighouse, Yorkshire HD6 4EJ
01484 713371

Wool-based, patterned and plain carpets. Fitting through retailers

Gaskell Carpets

Wheatfield Mill, Rishton, Blackburn, Lancashire BB1 4NU
01254 885566

Wool carpets in patterns and plains. Fitting through retailers

General George Carpets

Call 01689 895000 for details

Branches throughout Scotland (see Allied Carpets for range details)

Interface Europe

Ashlyms Hall, Chesham Road, Berkhamsted, Hertfordshire
HP4 2ST
01442 285000

Heuga carpet tiles in patterns and plains

Lyle Carpets

Tollpark Road, Wardpark East, Cumbernauld G68 0LW
01236 738211

Wool and man-made carpets in plains and heathers. Fitting through retailers

Natural Flooring Direct

PO Box 8104, London SE16 4ZA
Call 0800 454721

Natural floor coverings in coir, jute, wool, sisal and seagrass. Plain and patterned weaves. Prices include underlay, fixing and fitting. Mail order and some stockists

Ryalux Carpets

Ensor Mill, Queensway, Castleton, Rochdale, Lancashire
OL11 2NU
01706 716000

Wool and man-made carpets in patterns and plains. Dye-to-order on some ranges and sizes. Fitting through retailers

Sanderson

112–120 Brompton Road, London SW3 1JJ
0171 584 3344

Wool and man-made carpets in patterns, semi-plains and plains. Made-to-order

Saraband Designs

Bath Road, Stroud, Gloucestershire GL5 5ND
01453 872579

Large range of wool, seagrass, sisal, coir and jute designs. Fitting through retailers

Shaw Carpets

PO Box 4, Darton, Barnsley, South Yorkshire S75 5NH
01226 390390

Wool and man-made carpets in patterns and plains. Fitting through retailers

Stoddard Templeton

Glenpatrick Road, Elderslie, Johnstone, Renfrewshire PA5 9UJ
01505 577000

Wool-based, patterns and plains. Fitting through retailers

Three Shires

2 Eastborough Court, Alliance Business Park, Attleborough Fields, Nuneaton CV11 6SD
01203 370365

Natural floor coverings in coir, seagrass, jute and sisal. Fitting available

Threshold Flooring

Vorda Works, Highworth, Swindon, Wiltshire SN6 7AJ
01793 764301

Natural floor coverings in jute, sisal and coir. Plain or tapestry-bound rugs from stock or made to order. Fitting through retailers

Tintawn

Curragh Carpets, Newbridge, Co Kildare, Ireland
01306 884451

Wool and man-made carpets and natural jute flooring. Patterns and plains available. Fitting through retailers

Tomkinson Carpets

PO Box 11, Duke Place, Kidderminster, Worcestershire
DY10 2JR
Call 0800 374429

Wool and man-made carpets in patterns and plains. Fitting through retailers

Woodward Grosvenor

Stourvale Mills, Green Street, Kidderminster, Worcestershire
DY10 1AT
01562 820020

Wool and wool mix carpets in patterns and plains. Made-to-order. Fitting through retailers

---

Carpet Styles

Axminster

Patterned carpets using up to 36 colours woven on traditional looms and called after the Devon company that first made them (although these days they're made by many different manufacturers).

Brussels Weave

Also known as loop pile, this style of weave is very hardwearing because it's made up of a series of loops.

Cut and Loop

A combination of cut pile and loops, giving the carpet a sculpted appearance. Quite hardwearing and generally only available in plain colours.

Cut Pile

Made of single upright tufts, this weave applies to a number of carpet types. Long cut (shag) pile is in single, upright tufts which, because of their length, tend to lie flat. Suitable for low-traffic areas like bedrooms. Short cut pile is the most common type of carpet and is quite hardwearing. Available in in velvet/velour (which has a very smooth pile, feels extra soft underfoot but can show footmarks) and Hard Twist (which is twisted to create a hardwearing carpet with a tight texture).

Tufted

A generic term for carpets that aren't woven. The fibre is inserted into a primary backing with dozens of sewing-machine style needles. The pile is then secured with adhesive and a secondary backing is added. These carpets are less expensive than woven versions but don't feel as dense or luxurious.

Wilton

Named after their original manufacturer, Wiltons are usually plain or have no more than about five colours in a small pattern. They're either cut or loop pile and the pile fibre (usually wool) is woven into the backing.

Carpet Care

- Use castors to protect your carpet from heavy furniture.

- Raise flattened pile by rubbing it gently with the edge of a coin.

- Move furniture from time to time and alter the 'traffic flow' of rooms to even out carpet wear.

- Re-using old underlay is a false economy unless it's in excellent condition – a proper base for a carpet will prolong its life and deaden sound.

- Blot spills immediately with kitchen roll. Then try a carpet shampoo or stain remover (follow manufacturer's instructions carefully). Never use salt on carpets as it will remain ingrained in the pile and create a damp area.

- Choose a carpet that's appropriate for the amount of 'traffic'. Hardwearing carpets are essential for areas like halls and living rooms. Medium to light wear are suitable for bedrooms. If you're carpeting your bathroom, remember to choose a type that can withstand damp conditions and water spills.

- If you opt for pale colours, or you have young children or pets, choose a carpet that's been stain-treated.

Natural Floor Coverings

These have become increasingly popular in recent years because they're reasonably priced (from around £12 a square metre) and suit contemporary or traditional decorating schemes. You can choose from natural beiges/browns or colours and there are a variety of textures – from bouclé to jacquard – to add interest. But remember that natural materials are not suitable for the kitchen and dining room, where dropped crumbs will collect in the matting; or in the bathroom, where moisture may make them drag or warp.

Coir

Derived from coconuts and the ideal low-cost flooring for hallways and stairs.

Jute

This isn't as hardwearing as sisal, but its softness makes it suitable for bedrooms.

Rush

Used as both a fitted floor covering and a matting. It can tolerate slightly damp conditions, making it suitable for conservatories and floors that aren't totally damp-proofed.

Sisal

Soft enough for bedrooms and tough enough for stairs. Available in a wide variety of weaves, including herringbone, twill and plain.

Vinyl and Tiles

Amtico

Call 0800 667766 for stockists and information

Top-of-the-range vinyl flooring imitating marble, wood and ceramic tiles. Also customized designs and one-offs. Fitting through retailers

Bonar and Flotex

High Holborn Road, Ripley, Derbyshire DES 3NT
01773 744121

Stain-resistant flooring for all areas of the home

Castlenau Tiles

175 Church Road, London SW13 9HR
0181 741 2452

Ceramic, stone, slate and terracotta tiles and mosaics. Made-to-order service. Installation available

Cristal Tiles

H & R Johnson Tiles, Highgate Tile Works, Brownhills Road, Tunstall, Stoke-on-Trent ST6 4JX
01782 575575

Ceramic, encaustic and geometric tiles. Vitrified, fully vitrified, and glazed tiles

Dennis Ruabon

Hafod Tileries, Ruabon, Wrexham, Clwyd LL14 6ET
01978 843484

Plain and decorative quarry tiles and clay pavers. Made-to-order service

Elon Tiles

66 Fulham Road, London SW3 6HH
0171 460 4600

Terracotta tiles in various shapes and some slate tiles

Fired Earth

Twyford Mill, Oxford Road, Adderbury, Oxfordshire OX17 3HP
01295 812088

Wide range of ceramic and terracotta tiles, as well as a natural floor coverings collection. Fitting available

First Floor

174 Wandsworth Bridge Road, London SW6 2UQ
0171 736 1123

Individual designs for linoleum, vinyl inlays and borders. Made-to-order to customer specifications. Fitting available

Forbo-Nairn

PO Box 1, Kirkcaldy, Fife KY1 2SB
01592 643777

Cushioned vinyl, vinyl and linoleum flooring

Gerflor

Call 01926 401500

Sheet and tile vinyl flooring in patterns, plains, cushioned and flexible

Just Tiles

86–88 Headley Road, Woodley, Reading, Berkshire RG5 4JE
01734 697774

Hand-made terracotta, marble, granite and ceramic tiles. Made-to-order service. Installation available

Marley Floors & Waterproofing

Dickley Lane, Lenham, Maidstone, Kent ME17 2DE
01622 854000

Luxury vinyl sheet floor coverings and floor tiles. Peel-and-stick adhesive or fitting through retailer

Naturestone

Crossways, Silwood Road, Sunninghill, Berkshire SL5 0PZ
01344 27617

Slate, limestone, quartzite and sandstone flooring. Nationwide delivery. Mail order. Installation available

Pennine Flooring Supplies (Northern Cork Supplies)

Unit 303, Phoenix Close, Haywood, Lancashire OL10 2JG
01706 627255

Natural, sanded or sealed cork floors. Pvc-protected and hardwood floors, including laminates and pre-finished parquet. Nationwide delivery. Mail order. Special orders

Robus Ceramics

Evington Park, Hastingleigh, Ashford, Kent TN25 5JH
01233 750330

Large selection of terracotta tiles and decorative inserts. Also range made from local clay. Special designs by commission. Nationwide delivery. Installation available

Siesta Cork Tiles

Unit 21, Tait Road, Croydon, Surrey CR0 2DP
0181 683 4055

Acrylic-sealed/pvc-surfaced cork tiles in a variety of colours. National delivery

Stonell

Forstal House, Belting, Paddock Wood, Kent TN12 4PY
01892 833500

Natural stone floors

The York Handmade Brick Co

Forest Lane, Alne, North Yorkshire YO6 2LU
01347 838881 (Southern office 01327 350278)

Traditional terracotta tiles made from Vale of York clay. Hand-made pavers, decorative edgings. Nationwide delivery. Made-to-order

Wellington Tile Company

Tone Industrial Estate, Milverton Road, Wellington, Somerset TA21 0AZ
01823 667242

Patterned and plain terracotta, clay and slate tiles. Also products for maintaining tiled floors

Wood, Laminate and Parquet

Bruce Hardwood Floors

185 Milton Park, Abingdon, Oxfordshire OX14 4SR
01235 862222

Hardwood, plank, strip and parquet flooring in oak and maple. Various colours. Installation available

Campbell Marson & Co

(Warehouse) Unit 34, Wimbledon Business Centre, Riverside Road, London SW17 0BA
0181 879 1909
(Showroom) 573 King's Road, SW6 2EB
0171 371 5001

Parquet, blocks, strip, boards and mosaic wood, laminate and solid pre-finished floors. Made-to-order parquetry. Installation available

4 Wood Floors

Unit B, Wellington Trading Estate, Wellington, Somerset
TA21 8ST
01823 660912

Solid traditional hardwood flooring in block, mosaic, solid strip and plank. Made-to-order service. Installation available

Heritage Woodcraft

Heritage House, Wheatfield Way, Hinckley, Leicestershire
LE10 1YG
01455 890800

Hardwood floors in blocks, strips, overlays, mosaics and panels. Custom-made designs. Nationwide delivery

Ikea

2 Drury Way, North Circular Road, London NW10 0TH
0181 208 5600

Good-value wood veneer and laminate flooring in various colours

Junckers

Wheaton Court Commercial Centre, Wheaton Road,
Witham, Essex CM8 3UJ
01376 517512

Pre-finished solid hardwood strip floors in a range of colours and thicknesses. 8mm overlay available especially for DIY installations. Range also includes versions with neoprene strips to give appearance of a ship's deck

Kahrs UK

Unit 1, Timberlaine Estate, Gravel Lane, Quarry Lane,
Chichester, West Sussex PO19 2FJ
01243 778747

Wood strip, parquet and mosaic flooring in various thicknesses and shades

Marvella

Call 01689 895000

Patterns (granite and marble) and plain laminate flooring. Made-to-order service. Fitting available. Stocked by Allied Carpets and General George

Osterman & Scheiwe UK

Osmo House, 26 Swakeleys Drive, Ickenham, Middlesex
UB10 8QD
01895 234899

Solid wood plank, strip, block, solid pre-finished and melamine laminate flooring in a range of colours and finishes. Also protective Osmo Colour Hardwax Oil and cleaner for wood and cork

Perstorp Flooring

Call 01608 646222

Pergo laminate flooring

Tarkett

PO Box 173, Blackthorne Road, Colnbrook, Slough SL3 0AZ
01753 684533

Wooden flooring suitable for DIY or professional installation

Victorian Wood Works

International House, London International Freight Terminal (LIFT), Temple Mills Lane, London E15 2ES
0181 985 8280

New floors from reclaimed timber. Worldwide service. Made-to-order, supply or supply and fit. Refinishing for old wooden floors

Wicanders

Amorim UK, Amorim House, Star Road, Partridge Green, Horsham, West Sussex RH13 8RA
01403 710001 for stockists

Wooden flooring in a variety of finishes and cork in a variety of colours

Wickes

0500 300 328 (freephone)

Solid parquet and pre-sealed tongue-and-groove parquet squares

Woodfloors & Woodstripping

60 Gould Road, Twickenham, Middlesex TW2 6RS
0181 893 3201

Block, strip, wide boards and parquet floors. Restoration and special effects. Supply, fit and repair in west London, south-west London and western home counties

Woodstock

Ponsharden, Falmouth, Cornwall TR10 8AB
01326 376555

Hardwood floors suitable for DIY installation, including easy-lay and tongue-and-groove strips. Hardwood machined to any size for restoration and replacement. Mail order. Nationwide delivery

---

Making the Right Choice

Vinyl, linoleum and cork are warm underfoot and provide a hardwearing and easily cleaned surface for kitchens, bathrooms and halls. Vinyl is available in sheets or tiles. Sheets cover large surface areas quickly and generally come in 3m or 4m widths, so you can get a seamless finish in most rooms. Vinyl or linoleum tiles are more expensive but you can use them to create your own pattern. Cork is relatively inexpensive, easy to lay yourself and hardwearing if it's properly sealed. Stone and ceramic tiles, wood and laminate floors provide a classic finish, but they're not a good idea for flat dwellers looking to reduce noise.

Measuring Up

For a rough guide to floor area, measure the length and width of the room/area at its widest points. Multiply the two figures and then, to find the area in square yards divide by nine. For a metric calculation just multiply the two figures together. Before you choose flooring, check whether the price is per square yard or square metre. A square yard is slightly less than a square metre so the flooring may appear to be cheaper than it is. For carpets and more expensive flooring, have a professional measurement before you buy as a skilled fitter can save you money by making economies (in ordering underlay, for instance). Underlay and fitting are expensive (typically £5 or more for every square metre of carpet you buy), so choose the most durable carpet you can afford.

---

8 • FIRES AND FIREPLACES

A fire becomes an immediate focal point for a room, as well as being a useful source of additional heat. Traditional marble and slate designs have a period feel, while wooden surrounds suit a town or country setting. And if you're looking for a more contemporary look, there are cast-iron, brass and metallic stoves – and you don't even need a chimney for some of them. Before you buy a fire, restore an existing fireplace or choose which fuel to use, get advice from the relevant association (see Fire Brigade) and remember to have your chimney checked.

Acquisitions

Acquisitions House, 24–26 Holmes Road, London NW5 3AB
0171 482 2949

Fireplaces, tiles and surrounds reproduced from original designs

Amazing Grate Trading Company

Unit 22, Springvale Industrial Estate, Cwmbran, Gwent
NP44 5BA
01633 875881

Fireplaces and fireplace furniture

Anglia Fireplaces & Design

Anglia House, Kendal Court, 1 Cambridge Road, Impington, Cambridgeshire CB4 4NU
01223 234713

Traditional and contemporary gas/solid fuel fires, fireplaces and stoves. Chimney work

Aurora Marble

Green Lea Mills, Cross Green Road, Dalton, Huddersfield HD5 9XX
01484 510470

Fireplaces and fireplace furniture

Baxi Heating

Bronedge Road, Bamber Bridge, Preston, Lancs PR5 6SN
01772 695555

Gas fire manufacturer. Wall/floor, combination boilers, Bermuda back boiler system. Wall heaters and solid fuel fires

Be Modern

Western Approach, South Shields, South Tyneside NE33 5QZ
0191 455 3571

Traditional fireplace surrounds and fireplace furniture

Big Tree Fire Surrounds

Units 1–3, Holbrook Avenue, Holbrook Industrial Estate, Owithorpe, Sheffield S20 3FF
01142 510242

Large range of fire surrounds

Calor Gas

Athena Drive, Tatchbrook Park, Warwickshire CV34 6RL
0345 661111

Calor-gas fires

Diligence International

Highbank House, Up Somborne, Stockbridge, Hampshire SO20 6QZ
01794 388335

French fires in contemporary designs and fireplace accessories

Dimplex

Millbrook, Southampton, Hampshire SO15 0AW
01703 777117

Gas and electric fires and coal/wood burning-effect stoves

Elgin & Hall

Adelphi House, Hunton, Bedale, North Yorkshire DL8 1LY
01677 450712

Traditional fireplaces

Energy Centres from British Gas Retail

Waverly Street, Long Eaton, Nottinghamshire NG10 1HT
0115 9466700 (for your local store call 0800 850 900)

Gas and electric fires, fire surrounds. Installation available

Eric N Parker Masonry

Boston Road, Holbeach, Spalding, Lincolnshire PE12 7LS
01406 422309

Traditional Adam-style fire surrounds in wood and marble. Metal fire frames, hearth plates and stone kits

Fire Style

158 Upminster Road, Upminster, Essex RM14 2RB
01708 454136

Marble fire surrounds, also hardwood, made-to-measure surrounds. Gas coal fires. Installation available

Flamewave Fires

104 Branbridges Road, East Peckham, Kent TN12 5HH
01622 872579

Solid fuel stoves, solid fuel convector boxes and gas convector boxes

Flavel-Leisure

Clarence Street, Leamington Spa, Warwickshire CV31 2AD
01926 427027

Gas fires

Focal Point Fires

Avon Trading Park, Christchurch, Dorset BH23 2BT
01202 499330

Gas fires and surrounds

Galaxy Fireplace Systems

8 Unicorn Park, Unicorn Park Avenue, Bristol BS4 4EX
0117 9777393

Gas and electric fires and surrounds

Gazco

Osprey Road, Sowton Industrial Estate, Exeter, Devon
EX2 7JG
01392 444030

Gas fires and stoves

Grate Glow Fires

Mill Lane, Old Swan, Liverpool L13 4AJ
0151 252 6610

Fuel-effect fires

Intamarble

Carrara House, 119–123 Anglesey Business Park, Littleworth Road, Hednesford, Staffordshire WS12 5NR
01543 877889

Marble surrounds and grates, wooden and resin surrounds, and fireplace accessories

Jetmaster Fires

Manor House Avenue, Millbrook, Southampton, Hampshire
SO15 0AW
01703 774000

Wood, coal, LPG and natural gas-burning fires

Jøtul Products

Falcon Road, Sowton Industrial Estate, Exeter, Devon EX2 7LF
01392 474057

Stoves and fireplaces

Lyme Regis Engineering

Millwey Industrial Estate, Axminster, Devon EX13 5HU

Gas, multi-fuel and wood-burning stoves

Magiglo

Freepost CU1283, Broadstairs, Kent CT10 2BR
01843 602345

Decorative gas fires in standard and non-standard sizes

Modus Design

16 The Warren, Radlett, Hertfordshire WD7 7DX
01923 210442

Fireplaces in contemporary designs for use with gas or solid fuel

Morso

4 Wychwood Court, Cotswold Business Village, London Road,
Moreton-in-Marsh, Gloucestershire GL56 0JQ
01608 652233

Cast-iron stoves

Neilson (T & J W)

76 Coburg Street, Leith, Edinburgh EH6 6HJ
0131 554 4704

Antique and reproduction chimney pieces. Gas and electric fires. Fireplaces

New World Domestic Appliances

New World House, Thelwall Lane, Warrington, Cheshire WA4 1NL
01925 627627

Gas fires

Ouzledale Foundry

PO Box 4, Long Ing, Barnoldswick, Colne, Lancashire BB8 6BN
01282 813235

Stoves for wood and solid fuel. Victorian-style fires

Robinson Willey

Mill Lane, Old Swan, Liverpool L13 4AJ
0151 228 9111

Gas fires and gas wall heaters

Roston Iron Foundry

Bromley Works, Mill Lane, Ellastone, Derbyshire DE6 2HF
01335 324368

Traditional and contemporary iron fireplaces

Samuel Heath & Sons

Cobden Works, Leopold Street, Birmingham B12 0UJ
0121 772 2303

Fire accessories

Selkirk Manufacturing

Bassett House, High Street, Banstead, Surrey SM7 2LZ
01737 353388

Manufacturers of chimney flues and gas-fire boxes

Stovax

Falcon Road, Sowton Industrial Estate, Exeter, Devon EX2 7LF
Stovax Classic Fireplaces 01392 474055
Stovax Multi-fuel Stoves 01392 474056

Fireplaces, stoves, tiles and surrounds in traditional designs. Fireplace accessories

Straxgas

Longfield Road, Sydenham Industrial Estate, Leamington Spa, Warwickshire CV31 1XB
01926 882233

Gas fires and surrounds

Suncrest Surrounds

2 Swan Road, South West Industrial Estate, Peterlee, County Durham SR8 2HS
0191 586 3241 for customer services

Fire surrounds and electric fires

The Hot Spot

53–55 High Street, Uttoxeter, Staffordshire ST14 7JQ
01889 565411

Range of stoves

Trident Systems

Industrial Unit 12, Lea Hall Enterprise Park, Armitage Road, Rugeley, Staffordshire WS15 1LH
(01889 578530) Freephone 0500 400 403 for customer services

Specialist powered-flue gas fires

Valor Heating

Wood Lane, Erdington, Birmingham B24 9QP
0121 373 8111

Gas fires and room heaters

Vermont Castings

Unit 3a, Osprey Court, Hawkfield Business Park, Bristol BS14 0BB
0117 9641234

Wood stoves, gas stoves, multi-fuel stoves and fire accessories

Wonderfire

Unit 3a, Osprey Court, Hawkfield Business Park, Bristol BS14 0BB
0117 9641234

Gas fires – can tailor-make designs to fit non-standard fireplaces

Woodcraft Manufacturing

Beckside Mills, Beckside Lane, Bradford BD7 2JX
01274 570689

Wooden fire surrounds

Worcestershire Woodworking

Arthur Drive, Hoo Farm Industrial Estate, Worcester Road, Kidderminster DY11 7RA
01562 820681

Traditional wooden fire surrounds

Fire Brigade
Approved Coal Merchant Scheme

Victoria House, Southampton Row, London WC1B 4DH
0171 405 1601

For details of your local approved coal merchants

Complete Heat

116 Tanners Drive, Blakelands, Milton Keynes MK14 5BP
01908 210110
Complete Heat Scotland
Main Street, Crossgates, Fife KY4 8DH
01383 610290

Independent organization covering complete chimney service including chimney MOTs, heating system design and installation, and emergency fumes call-out service. Spare parts service

CORGI

1 Elmwood, Chineham Business Park, Crockford Lane, Basingstoke RG24 8WG
01256 372200

The Council for Registered Gas Installers maintains a register of competent gas installers in the UK. Regulates companies who fit gas fires and ensures proper safety standards are adhered to

Gas Consumers Council

Abford House, 15 Wilton Road, London SW1V 1LT (head office)
0645 060 708 (for regional offices)

Watchdog organization representing the UK's gas users

National Association of Chimney Sweeps/National Association of Chimney Lining Engineers

St Mary's Chambers, 19 Station Road, Stone, Staffordshire
ST15 8JP
0800 833464

For advice on chimney maintenance and details of local chimney sweeps

National Fireplace Association

6th Floor, The McLaren Building, 35 Dale End, Birmingham
B4 7LN
0121 200 1310

For a list of fireplace retailers

Society of British Gas Industries

36 Holly Walk, Leamington Spa, Warwickshire CV32 4LY
01926 334357

For information and advice on different gas fires and requirements for installation, chimneys and safety

Solid Fuel Association

The Old School House, Church Street, Sutton-in-Ashfield,
Nottinghamshire NG17 1AE

For guidance on types of solid fuel and advice on opening up your fireplace

Victorian Society

1 Priory Gardens, Bedford Park, London W4 1TT
0181 994 1019

Eight-page guide on restoring Victorian and Edwardian fireplaces available for £3

Choosing the Right Design

- Remember to take into account the dimensions and furnishing style of your room – an ornate design may overpower a smaller room and heavily patterned tiles and coloured fire surrounds will restrict decorating schemes.

- Fireplace showrooms and manufacturers can advise you on the amount of heat different materials and styles give out – an important factor if this is the room's primary source of heat.

- If you're using an existing chimney, the fire needs to be compatible with its size and construction. If not, you can opt for a freestanding stove, open-front gas fire with powered flue or a hearth-standing glass-front model with balanced flue.

- Remember to check if you live in a smoke-control area, as this will restrict your choice of fuels.

- Many showrooms have videos showing different settings to help you come to a decision. Request a home visit for on-the-spot advice and ask to see pictures of fireplaces the retailer has installed.

Safety Pointers

- If you're working with an old chimney, ask for a smoke test and have the chimney examined for defects.

- Damaged chimneys should be re-lined and advice and free literature are available from the National Association of Chimney Lining Engineers. The Solid Fuel Association will also advise on chimney repairs. You'll also need to have the chimney swept.

- If you're choosing a gas fire, check that it carries a CE mark to indicate that it complies with European safety standards and make sure you have it installed by a CORGI-registered installer.

- Gas fires need an annual service, so keep a note of the fitter's phone number.

- Make sure the gas fire has automatic ignition and a flame supervision device that cuts off the gas if the flame goes out.

- An oxygen depletion sensor is a good safety feature as it will cut off the gas if there is an unsafe build-up of carbon monoxide.

- Check that the controls are easy to operate.

- Install smoke alarms and CO detectors and make sure the room is properly ventilated. Keep flammable materials like rugs well away from the fire and make sure you buy and use a fireguard.

9 • LIGHTING

Good lighting can make all the difference to a room, improving less than perfect paintwork or worn furnishings. When you're planning major redecoration, give lighting the same consideration as colour schemes or new furniture, and if you're looking for a quick fix, adding more table lamps, a couple of task lights or uplighters, or even changing harsh bright bulbs for lower wattage versions can make all the difference.

Acres Farm

Bradfield, Reading, Berkshire RG7 6JH
01734 744305

Candleshades. Mail order available

Ann's Lighting

34a/b Kensington Church Street, London W8 4HA
0171 937 5033

Traditional light fittings. Lampshades made to order. Conversions and repairs

Bella Figura

Decoy Farm, Old Church Road, Melton, Suffolk IP13 6DH
01394 461111

Traditional decorative lighting, silk shades, chandeliers, standard/table lamps, wall lights. Mail order available

Bhs

Call 0171 262 3288 for local stockists

Brilliant designs, including chandeliers, shades, lamps and pendants, at good-value prices

Bromleighs

68 Chapel Road, West Bergholt, Essex CO6 3JA
01206 241434

Period and decorative light switches and sockets in brass, chrome, iron and hardwood. Mail order available

Christopher Wray

600 King's Road, London SW6 2YW
0171 736 8434

Huge range of period lighting, including Tiffany-style shades and chandeliers. Mail order available

David Hunt Lighting

Tilemans Lane, Shipston-on-Stour, Warwickshire CV36 4HP
01608 661590

Traditional, classical and contemporary

Dernier & Hamlyn

28–30 South Bank Business Centre, Ponton Road, Vauxhall, London SW8 5BL
0171 622 1221

Designs based on eighteenth- and nineteenth-century fittings

Elite Lighting

7 Goodwood Parade, Upper Elmers End Road, Beckenham, Kent BR3 3QZ
0181 639 0050

Decorative traditional and contemporary lighting – chandeliers, wall brackets and pendants. Mail-order brochure available

Furniture Union

46 Beak Street, London W1R 3DA
0171 287 3424

Stylish contemporary light fittings. Mail order available

Habitat

Call 0645 334455

Extensive range of low-key lighting

House of Fraser

Call 0171 963 2236 customer inquiries

Lighting at competitive prices

Ikea

Brent Park, 2 Drury Way, North Circular Road, London NW10 0TH
Call 0181 208 5600 for branches

Huge range of light fittings and bulbs, including halogen fittings

John Cullen Lighting

585 King's Road, London SW6 2EH
0171 371 5400

Specialists in lighting design, supply and installation

John Lewis

278–306 Oxford Street, London W1A 1EX
0171 629 7711

Well-stocked lighting department, including bases, fittings and shades

Jones (Antique Lighting)

194 Westbourne Grove, London W11 2RH
0171 229 6866

Victorian, Edwardian, Art Nouveau and Art Deco lighting

Kensington Lighting Company

59 Kensington Church Street, London W8 4HA
0171 938 2405

Traditional light fittings. Lampshades made to order – from Anne's Showroom 0171 937 5033

Leading Lights (John Gibbons)

Call 01386 831245 for a brochure (mail order)

Hand-crafted wall lights in traditional designs. Also planning service

Lights on Broadway

17 Jerdan Place, London SW6 1BF
0171 610 0100

Reproduction Art Nouveau period lighting, darkened solid brass and traditional light fittings all at good-value prices

Lion, Witch & Lampshade

89 Ebury Street, London SW1 9QU 0171 730 1774
Broxborne Barn, High Street, Northleach, Cheltenham, Glos GL55 3EF 01451 860 855

Large range of traditional designs. Converts old lights to suit modern electrical requirements. Shades, wall brackets and chandeliers restored and made to order

Mr Light

279 King's Road, London SW3 5EW
0171 352 8398

Large range of contemporary lighting. Mail order available

Olivers Lighting Company

6 The Broadway, Crockenhill, Swanley, Kent BR8 8JH
01322 614224

Period light switches and co-ordinating sockets, and ceiling roses. Mail order available

Period Brass Lights

9a Thurloe Place, Brompton Road, London SW7 2RZ
0171 589 8305

Chandeliers and period lighting. Installation available. Mail order available

Ryness Electrical Supplies Ltd

34–41 White Lion Street, London N1 9PQ
0171 278 8993

Huge stock of fittings for house and garden. Household appliances and light bulbs. Mail order available

Suzie Clayton

2 St Margaret's Business Centre, Moor Mead Road, Twickenham TW1 1JS
0181 607 9704

Lamps and shades

The Lamp Gallery

355 New King's Road, London SW6 4RJ
0171 736 6188

Authentic antique light fittings, including Victorian, Edwardian, Art Nouveau and Art Deco

Tulissio de Beaumont

283 Lillie Road, London SW6 7LL
0171 385 0156

Period lighting, including chandeliers, lamps and wall brackets

---

Choosing Bulbs

- Tungsten filament bulbs (GLS) are the most common light source. Available in pear, golfball and candle shapes, they can be clear, opaque or pastel. Choose crown-silvered or reflector versions to reduce glare.

- Bulbs have bayonet or screw fittings – always check before you buy.

- Fluorescent tubes, suitable for work areas like kitchens, now come in smaller energy-saving versions.

- Tungsten halogen bulbs are more expensive, but they last much longer than ordinary bulbs.

- For areas like halls, where lighting is in constant use, replace standard bulbs with low-energy versions. They last up to ten times longer and use 80 per cent less electricity.

The Right Effect

- Overhead Lighting
  This provides 'ambient' or background lighting to soften shadows, reduce contrast and create a comfortable environment. It's usually in the form of a pendant or shade from the ceiling, although wall-mounted uplighters are a softer alternative. Try reducing the wattage of the bulb if the light still feels too harsh. A dimmer switch will give more flexibility.

- Side Lights
  You can create a warmer atmosphere and enought light for reading by adding standard or table lamps in different corners of the room. Or try free-standing uplighters for a more contemporary feel.

- Accent Lighting
  This is ideal for picking out objects, such as pictures or ornaments. Make sure the light isn't too overpowering for the object you want to highlight.

- Task Lighting
  This is essential for reading and study and the best option is a directional spotlight that can be positioned on a desk or wall.

10 • ACCESSORIES

One of the quickest ways to update a room is to change the details – a new duvet cover, crisp cotton tablecloth or set of brightly coloured glasses. Our round-up of accessories includes glassware, tableware and household linens in a range of price points, including budget and factory finds.

Glassware

Allders

PO Box 359, Centre Tower, Whitgift Centre, Croydon, Surrey CR9 1NN
0181 681 5232

Good-value casual and formal glassware

Argos

Call 01908 600161

Inexpensive glass sets

Boots

Call 0115 950 6111

Classic designs at good prices

Cargo Homeshops

Call 0990 134950

Casual and formal designs

Dartington Crystal

Call 01805 626262 for stockists

Contemporary and classic glasses, jugs and vases

Edinburgh Crystal

Call 01968 672244 for stockists

Cut crystal and giftware

Grand Illusions

2–4 Crown Road, St Margarets, Twickenham, Middx TW1 3EE
0181 744 1046

Unusual glassware and accessories. Mail order available

Habitat

Call 0645 334433

Everyday glassware in interesting designs

Harrods

87–135 Brompton Road, Knightsbridge, London SW1X 7XL
0171 730 1234

Vast selection of glassware

Heal's

196 Tottenham Court Road, London W1P 9LD
0171 636 1666

Modern classics for formal and everyday use. Lots of coloured glasss

Ikea

2 Drury Way, North Circular Road, London NW10 0TH
Call 0181 208 5600 for branches

Low prices for everyday drinking glasses

J G Durand & Cie

Call 0171 316 0014 for stockists

Glasses and toughened glass cooking items in Cristal D'Arques, Luminarc, Arcoflam and Arcopal ranges

John Jenkins & Sons

Call 01730 821811 for stockists

Classic hand-made designs

John Lewis

278–306 Oxford Street, London W1A 1EX
0171 629 7711

Wide range of casual and formal glass, including extensive range of vases and accessories

Liberty

214–220 Regent Street, London W1R 6AH
0171 734 1234

Lots of casual and formal glassware plus designer sections. Good range of coloured glass

Marks & Spencer

Call 0171 935 4422 for branches and catalogue

Formal and everyday designs

Mulberry Hall

Stonegate, York, YO1 2AW
01904 620736

Fine crystal, china and giftware

Royal Doulton Crystal

Call 01782 292292 for stockists

Classic crystal glasses and giftware

Selfridges

400 Oxford Street, London W1A 1AB
0171 629 1234

Wide choice, including vases, glasses and accessories

The General Trading Company

144 Sloane Square, London SW1X 9BL
0171 730 0411

Casual and formal ranges. Repairs undertaken

The Pier

Call 0171 351 7100 for branches

Cheerful, inexpensive designs

Types of Glass

Handmade

Glasses are mouth-blown and individually made. Can be coloured and decorated and tend to be expensive.

Factory Made

Cheaper to buy, less intricate but can still have fine details. Factory methods are pressing (for some glasses, bowls and plates) or machine blowing (where the neck of an item is narrower than the body).

Soda Glass

Everyday glass used for cheaper tumblers and vases. Contains a maximum 10 per cent lead.

Lead Crystal

Contains minimum 24 per cent lead (so is heavier than ordinary glass), and is exceptionally clear and clean. (Crystalline glass contains between 18 and 24 per cent lead.)

Cut Glass

Lead crystal glass which is cut using a diamond impregnated cutting wheel – traditional patterns include lace, diamond, fan and flute. Beware cheap imitations!

Recycled Glass

Often with a greenish tinge, usually heavy, everyday designs with lots of bubbles and 'flaws' which add to the casual feel.

China and Crystal Factory Shops

- **Denby Factory Shop**
  Denby Visitor Centre, Denby Road, Derbyshire DE5 8NX.
  Call 01773 570684
  Sells Dartington Crystal as well as Denby tableware

- **Dartington Crystal Factory Shop and Visitor Centre**
  Torrington, North Devon
  Call 01805 626269 for tour details

- **Edinburgh Crystal Visitor Centre**
  Penicuik, Midlothian
  Call 01968 675128 for tour details

- **Portmeirion Factory Shop**
  Normacott Road, Longton, Stoke-on-Trent ST3 1PW
  Call 01782 326412

- **Royal Doulton Factory Shop**
  Nile Street, Burslem, Stoke-on-Trent ST6 2AJ
  Call 01782 292292
  Sells china and crystal

- **Royal Worcester**
  Severn Street, Worcester WR1 2NE
  Call 01905 23221

- **Spode**
  Church Street, Stoke-on-Trent ST4 1BX
  Call 01782 744011

- **Wedgwood Factory Shop**
  King Street, Fenton, Stoke-on-Trent ST4 3DQ
  Call 01782 316161

China and Tableware

Cargo Homeshops

Call 0990 134950 for branches or to order

Casual tableware, including Italian designs and boxed sets

Cloverleaf

Arkwright Road, Groundwell, Swindon, Wilts SN2 5BB
01793 724556

Ceramic storage, cooking and serving ware and classic Cornish Blue and Cornish Green tableware

Debenhams

334–348 Oxford Street, London W1A 1DF
0171 408 4444

Large range of formal and informal tableware and good-value boxed sets

Denby Pottery

Denby, Derbyshire DE5 8NX
01773 740700

Classic patterned and plain styles in traditional and contemporary shapes

Habitat

Call 0645 334433 for branches

Modern tableware with a Mediterranean feel

Harrods

87–135 Brompton Road, Knightsbridge, London SW1X 7XL
0171 730 1234

A vast range of styles and patterns under one roof. Worth a visit if you're trying to choose a dinner service design

Heal's

196 Tottenham Court Road, London W1P 9LD
0171 636 1666

Modern, quirky designs. Lots of hand-painted kitchenware

House of Fraser

Call 0171 963 2236 for stores

Fine china and casual ranges

Ikea

2 Drury Way, North Circular Road, London NW10 0TH
0181 208 5600

Bargain-priced boxed sets

John Lewis

278–306 Oxford Street, London W1A 1EX
0171 629 7711

Wide choice of casual and formal ranges

Johnson Brothers

Barlaston, Stoke-on-Trent ST12 9ES
01782 204141

Formal and informal tableware

Liberty

214 Regent Street, London W1R 6AH
0171 734 1234

Wide selection of casual and formal ware. Rosenthal and Villeroy & Boch in-store shops

Michael Johnson Ceramics

81 Kingsgate Road, London NW6 4JY
0171 624 2493

Gien and Raynaud Porcelain from France

Mulberry Hall

Stonegate, York YO1 2AW
01904 620736

China, crystal and giftware

Portmeirion

London Road, Stoke-on-Trent ST4 7QQ
01782 744721

Classic botanical and floral table- and cookware

Royal Doulton
(also Royal Crown Derby, Royal Albert, Minton, John Beswick)

Minton House, London Road, Stoke-on-Trent ST4 7QD
01782 292292

Formal and everyday ranges. Wide selection of classic and contemporary designs

Royal Worcester

Severn Street, Worcester WR1 2NE
Call 01905 23221 for stockists

Classic fine bone china

Selfridges

400 Oxford Street, London W1A 1AB
0171 629 1234

Formal and informal designs

Spode

Church Street, Stoke-on-Trent ST4 1BX
Call 01782 744011 for stockists

Classic china designs. Site includes factory shop

The General Trading Company

144 Sloane Street, London SW1X 9BL
0171 730 0411

Fine china and casual dining ware

The Pier

Call 0171 351 7100 for branches

Hand-painted Mediterranean-style designs

The Source

26–40 Kensington High Street, London W8 4PF
0171 937 2626

Wide range of modern, inexpensive designs

Thomas Goode & Co

19 South Audley Street, London W1Y 6BN
0171 499 2823

Exquisite china and glass ranges – good for giftware.

Villeroy & Boch

Call 0181 871 0011

Modern and classic designs

Wedgwood
(also Mason's Ironstone)

Barlaston, Stoke-on-Trent ST12 9ES
01782 204141

Classic Wedgwood china, as well as Mason's Ironstone and Johnson Brothers. Factory shop on the site

---

Types of Tableware

Earthenware

Inexpensive, widely available and made of a clay base with a thick glaze. It feels quite heavy and solid, but has a tendency to chip easily.

Porcelain

Fine and delicate-looking, but actually much more durable than earthenware. Can be decorated with intricate designs.

Bone china

A smooth translucent finish makes this the classic choice for formal tableware. But looks can be deceptive – it has added bone ash for strength and should stand up to frequent use. Expensive, but a good investment.

Matchmakers

Breaking a favourite piece of china is bad enough, but if the set has been discontinued, it can be a disaster. Tablewhere is a china-matching service that stocks thousands of discontinued patterns from leading manufacturers. If the piece isn't in stock, the company will search for it on your behalf and it claims an 85 per cent success rate. Call 0171 706 4586. Lovers of Blue and White supplies a wide range of old china by post, including classic blue and white patterns by Adams, Spode and Booths. Regular catalogues contain clear descriptions of each piece, including its condition. If you're collecting a dinner service, let the company know and they'll keep you posted when new pieces come in. Call 01763 853800.

Household Linens

Bhs

Call 0171 262 3288 for branches

Extensive range of towels and colourful bed linen with matching ready-made curtains and accessories. Excellent children's range

Christy

Call 0161 954 9322 for stockists

Luxurious towels in lots of colours

Cologne & Cotton

Call 01926 332573 for branches and catalogue

Classic French-style bed linen, waffle towels, bathmats and robes. Also stocks table linen

Cramlington Textiles

Call 01670 713434 for stockists

Extensive range of bed linen

Crown Wallcoverings

Call 01254 704213 for stockists

Co-ordinated range of bed linen, borders and wallcoverings

Descamps

Call 0171 235 6957 for mail order and catalogues

High-quality French bed linen and towels and Petit Descamps children's range

Divertimenti

Call 0171 386 9911 for catalogue and branches

Professional range of kitchen linens

Dorma

Call 0161 251 4400 for stockists

Bed linen and co-ordinating accessories

Early's of Witney

Witney Mill, Witney, Oxfordshire OX8 5EB
01993 703131

Large range of blankets

Habitat

Call 0645 334433 for local branches

Contemporary bed linen, towels and table linen

Hamilton McBride

Call 01282 858200 for stockists

Good-value bed linen in contemporary designs

Homestyle

Call 0990 133610 for branches

Good-value bed linen

House of Fraser

Call 0171 963 2236 for branches

Extensive range of bed linen, towels and table linen

Ikea

2 Drury Way, North Circular Road, London NW10 0TH
0181 208 5600

Bed linen, table linen and towels in colourful designs

Index Extra

Call 0800 401080

Good selection of plain and patterned bed linen

Jane Churchill

151 Sloane Street, London SW1X 9BX
0171 7309847

Patterned and co-ordinated bed linen and accessories

J C Penney

Call 0800 334488

Popular American brand now available by mail order in the UK. Vast range of co-ordinated bed linen and curtains, towels and bath mats

John Lewis

Call 0171 629 7711

One-stop shopping for bed linen, table linen and towels. Extensive range and good-value own brand (Jonelle)

Kennard & Co

Call 01734 712046 for catalogue

Classic bed linen in sizes up to super king

Keys of Clacton

132 Old Road, Clacton-on-Sea, Essex CO15 3AJ
Call 01255 432518 for catalogue

Extensive range, including made-to-order and special sizes

Laura Ashley

Call 0900 622116 for branches and catalogue

Traditional bed linen in pretty designs

Malabar

Call 0171 501 4200

Cotton bedspreads in vivid Indian checks

Marks & Spencer

Call 0171 935 4422

Good quality household linens. Range includes non-iron pure cotton bed linen

McCord

Call 01793 435553 for catalogue

Bed linen and kitchen textiles, including colourful Provençal range

MFI

Call 0500 192192 for branches

Good-value bed linen in Home Works ranges

Monogrammed Linen Shop

168 Walton Street, London SW3 2JL
0171 589 4033

Exquisite range of table and bed linen, including plenty of embroidered items

New England Direct

Call 01527 577111 for catalogue

American quilts and throws

Next Interiors

Call 0345 100500 for branches and catalogue

Good range of towels and lots of bright cotton bed linen, including easy-iron range

Nimbus

Call 0800 585069 for stockists

Extensive bed linen range

Pret à Vivre

Call 0171 328 4500

Table linen

Pukka Palace

The Market Hall, Craven Arms, Shropshire SY7 9NY
Call 0345 666660 for catalogue

Towels, table linen, quilts and throws

Rectella

Railway Road, Chorley, Lancashire PR6 0HL
01257 272211

Co-ordinated bed linen, borders and curtains. Good children's range

Sanderson Bed Linen Collection

112–120 Brompton Road, London SW3 1JJ
0171 584 3344

Sophisticated designs and classic florals

The Source

26–40 Kensington High Street, London W8 4PF
0171 937 2626

Excellent-value range of cotton bed linen, including Egyptian cotton and Indian waffle weave. Also towels and table linen

The White Company

Call 0171 385 7988 for mail order

Traditional white bed linen, towels and table linen

Turquaz

Call 0171 924 3003 for mail order, 0171 924 6894 for stockists

Bed and table linen in bright checks and naturals

Yves Delorme

PO Box 157, Aylesbury, Buckinghamshire HP19 3XZ
01296 394980

Pretty and luxurious bed linen

What's What in the Linen Cupboard

Linen and cotton are the two most luxurious fabrics for bed and table linen. They cost more but are a practical buy because you can wash them at higher temperatures and linen is particularly durable. Egyptian cotton is highly prized because it is strong and durable and maintains its crisp texture after countless washes. Percale is a type of weave that feels soft and luxurious and it can be made of either cotton or a polyester/cotton combination. Anything with polyester in it tends to be less expensive and, although it can feel quite scratchy and isn't as cool as pure cotton, its benefits include fast drying and easy or no ironing.

Budget Buys

The linen department is one of the best places to pick up sale bargains. Look for neutral white or cream oddments – they're often sold singly and will fit in with any colour scheme. Check for damaged seams, missing buttons or flaws in the weave before you buy. Provided you can sew a seam you can make your own bed or table linen – most department stores sell sheeting, cotton suitable for duvet covers and finer weaves for tablecloths. If you're making your own bed linen, take measurements carefully and allow a certain amount of slack to make changing the sheets less of a struggle! If you want to brighten up old bed linen, or match something to a room scheme you could always use a Dylon Machine Dye – there are 22 shades to choose from and they're suitable for dyeing cotton, linen and viscose in the washing machine.

Armchair Shopping

For clever accessories and unusual finishing touches, try the following mail-order companies:

Appalachia

Call 01727 836796

Folk art accessories

Epoch

01242 524 000

Wacky accessories and gifts in brilliant colours

House

01258 454884

Selection of home accessories

In Particular

0701 0702 027

Decorative accessories from British designers

Lakeland Plastics

015394 88100

Gadgets, fkitchen and tableware, plus a separate storage catalogue

McCord

0990 535455

Large range of accessories

New England Direct

01527 577111

Original American products

Nice Irma's by Post

0181 343 7610

Soft furnishings and unusual accessories

Ocean

0800 132 985

Quirky gifts and accessories

Past Times

01993 770440

Gifts and accessories inspired by the past

Scotts of Stow

0990 449111

Kitchen and home accessories

Shaker

0171 724 7672

Simple Shaker-style accessories

The Art Room

Call 01993 770444

Prints and frames

The Catalogue from Presents Direct

0171 371 7017

Wide range of gifts and accessories

Touch Design

01725 552888

Stylish ideas for the home

The Royal Academy of Arts

0151 708 0555

Quirky selection of art-inspired gifts

11 • ARCHITECTURAL FEATURES AND PERIOD DETAILS

Whether you're looking for period-style coving, a traditional beam or a slimline vertical radiator in a bright contemporary colour, there's a supplier who can help. Many of the companies listed also undertake restoration and repair work, or can advise you on finding the right specialist for the job in hand.

Acova Radiators

30 Rowland Way, Hoo Farm Industrial Estate, Kidderminster
DY11 7RA
01562 753001

Space-saving vertical and horizontal radiators in a range of unusual colours and designs

Aristocast Originals

14a Orgreave Close, Dore House Industrial Estate,
Handsworth, Sheffield S13 9NP
0114 2690900

Co-ordinated plasterwork features, including fire surrounds, cornices and ceiling roses

Artisan Period & Victorian Joinery

Grange Farm, Buxshalls Hill, Lindfield, Sussex
01444 484491

Hand-made doors, windows, panelling and fitted and freestanding cupboards

Bisque

15 Kingsmead Square, Bath, Somerset BA1 2AE
01225 469244

Radiators in sleek contemporary designs and a range of colours

Bleasdale (Spirals)

394 Caledonian Road, London N1 1DW
0171 609 0934

Wrought-iron stairs, railings, balconies and room dividers

Blue Hawk

Pasture Lane, Ruddington, Nottingham NG11 6AG
0115 9846212

Plaster coving, borders, cornices, corbels and ceiling roses

Book Backs

The Manor Bindery, Fawley, Hampshire SO45 1BB
01703 894488

False book backs to disguise cupboards, doors, TVs and other electrical equipment

British Museum Company

46 Bloomsbury Street, London WC1B 3QQ
0171 323 1234

Wall reliefs and statuary replicas of items from the British Museum

Classic Interiors

Roberts House, 17 Moor Road, Broadstone, Dorset
BH18 8AZ
01202 694997

Infill for transforming plain cornices into decorative coving. Decorative plasterwork, plus restoration and match service

Classic Radiator Cover Company

Unit 215, Mountain Ash Industrial Estate, Mountain Ash, Mid Glamorgan CF45 4EY
01443 477824

Wide selection of radiator covers

Copley Decor Mouldings

Leyburn Business Park, Leyburn, North Yorkshire DL8 5QA
01969 623410

Polyurethane mouldings, including ceiling roses, cornices and door pediments. Brochure and mail order available

Elite Stairs

Unit 7, Blue Lias Marina Estate, Rugby Road, Stockton, Rugby, Warwickshire CV23 8HN
01926 812060

Traditional and contemporary spiral staircases

Gifford Mead

Furniture Cave, 533 King's Road, London SW10 0TZ
0171 352 6008

Stair spindles, newel and gallery posts and handrails

Haddonstone

The Forge House, Church Lane, East Haddon, Northampton NN6 8DB
01604 770711

Bespoke joinery, including fireplaces, door surrounds, panelling, moulding, bookcases and staircases. Also reproduction stonework

Hodkin & Jones

Callywhite Lane, Dronfield, Sheffield S18 6XP
01246 290890

Fibrous plaster mouldings, including cornices, ceiling roses, panel mouldings, architraves, columns, corbels and classical busts

House of Brass

45–47 Milton Street, Nottingham NG1 3EZ
0115 9475430

Brass door furniture, electrical accessories and bell pushes. Also bedsteads and hearthware. Mail order available

Jali

Albion Works, Church Lane, Barham, Canterbury CT4 6QS
01227 831710

Ready-to-paint MDF shelf trims and decorative details

J Price & Sons

118 Guernsey Road, Liverpool L13 6RY
0151 220 2839

Victorian-style brass stair rods

Kensington Spirals

27 Ribocon Way, Progress Park, Leagrave, Luton LU4 9TR
01582 491171

Spiral staircases

Market Square

Wing Farm, Longbridge Deverill, Warminster, Wiltshire
BA12 7DD
01985 841041

Wood panelling supplied in component form in pine or stained finishes. Ornamental plate shelves

MHS Radiators

35 Nobel Square, Burnt Mills Industrial Estate, Basildon, Essex
SS13 1LT
01268 591010

Traditional-style radiators, including Victorian designs

Muriel Short Designs

Elmbridge Road, Cranleigh, Surrey GU6 8LW
01483 271211

Polyurethane mouldings, including cornices, niches, corbels and wall lights

Oakleaf Reproductions

Ling Bob Mill, Main Street, Wilsden Bradford, West Yorkshire
BD15 0JP
01535 272878

Cottage craft range of oak beams, joists, corbels, plate racks, fireplaces and accessories

Rudloe Stone Works

Lower Rudloe Farm, Box, Wiltshire SN13 0PB
01225 811545

Bath and Portland stone fireplaces

Solair

Smeaton Road, Churchfields, Salisbury, Wiltshire SP2 7NQ
01722 323036

Reproduction louvres, columns, dormer windows, cupolas, canopies and porches

Stevensons of Norwich

Roundtree Way, Norwich NR7 8SQ
01603 400824

Large range of plaster and GRP mouldings. Custom-made designs and restoration work

Stylecast Trading Company

18 Goodrich Avenue, Perton, West Midlands WV6 7UL
0121 522 4664

Cast-iron ceiling racks and laundry pulleys

The Bulbeck Foundry

Reach Road, Burwell, Cambridgeshire CB5 0AH
01638 743153

Reproduction lead statuary, fountains and wall plaques

The Cast Iron Shop

394 Caledonian Road, London N1 1DW
0171 609 0934

Metal spiral staircases and balconies

The Domestic Paraphernalia Company

Unit 15, Marine Business Centre, Dock Road, Lytham, Lancashire FY8 5AJ
01253 736334

Victorian-style hanging clothes airers

The London Crown Glass Company

Twin Archway, Elizabeth Road, Henley-on-Thames RG9 1RJ
01491 413227

Hand-blown window glass for period buildings

The London Door Company

0800 387905

Hand-made internal and external doors and room dividers

Troika Architectural Mouldings

Troika House, 41 Clun Street, Sheffield S4 7JS
0114 2753222

Cornices, ceiling and wall decorations, beam casings and door and window surrounds

Ventrolla

11 Hornbeam Square South, Harrogate, North Yorkshire
HG2 8NB
01423 870011

Repair and restoration of sash windows

Architectural Salvage

Andy Thornton Architectural Antiques

Victoria Mills, Stainland Road, Greetland, Halifax, West Yorkshire HX4 8AD
01422 377314

This huge warehouse packed full of architectural antiques has become such a tourist attraction that they've begun charging £1 entrance fee at weekends and bank holidays (refundable if you buy something). Also manufacturers' reproduction furniture, glass, metalwork, brass fittings and lighting

Antique Buildings

Alfold Road, Dunsfold, Surrey GU8 4NP
01483 200477

Old oak beams, hand-made bricks and walling stone. Architectural and design consultancy

Bathing Beauties

43 Muswell Hill Road, Muswell Hill, London N10 3JB
0181 365 2794

Original bathroom fittings

Clayax Yorkstone

Derry Hill, Menston, Leeds LS29 6AZ
01943 878351

Traditional stone bricks to blend in with period properties

Reclamation Services

Catbrain Quarry, Painswick Beacon, Painswick, Gloucestershire GL6 6SU
01452 814064

Oak-block flooring, beams and trusses, architectural features and on-site facility for making stone mullions and fireplaces and restoring old stone ornaments. Garden statuary

Staffordshire Architectural Salvage

Stain House, Skidmore Road, Coseley, Bilston, West Midlands WV14 8SE
01902 401053

Old stonework and statuary, flagstones and bricks. Oak, elm and pitch pine flooring

The London Architectural Salvage & Supply Company

St Michael's Church, Mark Street, London EC2A 4ER
0171 739 0448

Large stocks of reclaimed period architectural details, including flooring, masonry, timber, lighting, bathroom and kitchen fittings, fences and gates and metalware and door furniture

Walcot Reclamation

108 Walcot Street, Bath BA1 5BG
01225 444404

Huge stocks of period furnishings and details, from old nails to entire panelled rooms. Period chimney pieces and fireplaces, old radiators, doors and bathroom furnishings. Restoration work

---

Treasure Seeking

Our continuing love affair with original and period features means that architectural salvage yards are not the bargain-hunters' paradise they once were, but you can still pick up real treasures at reasonable prices if you hunt around. Building supply yards and your Yellow Pages should have information about local architectural salvage companies. Skips can turn up finds from time to time, and it's always worth checking at your local tip (although you shouldn't take anything without asking the staff in charge).

---

12 • OUTDOOR SUPPLIES

Gardens should be treated as an extra room – a place to entertain friends and eat alfresco when the weather is warm, and there are plenty of ways to 'decorate' this outdoor space. Our listing includes everything from pergolas and gazebos to shutters, statues and garden furniture. We've also included a separate listing of conservatory companies, if you'd like to turn part of your garden into a year-round area for relaxing and entertaining.

Agriframes

Charlwoods Road, East Grinstead, West Sussex RH19 2HG
01342 310000

Pergolas, gazebos and other garden frames

Allibert

Berry Hill Industrial Estate, Droitwich, Worcestershire WR9 9AB
01905 795796

Lightweight garden furniture in a range of colours

Baileys

The Engine Shed, Ashburton Industrial Estate, Ross-on-Wye, Herefordshire HR9 7BW
01989 563 015

Garden antiques, including old cast-iron urns

Barnsley House

Barnsley House, Barnsley, Nr Cirencester, Gloucestershire
GL7 5EE
01285 740561

Classical furniture designs in wrought iron

Burgon & Ball

La Plata Works, Holme Lane, Sheffield S6 4JY
0114 2338262

Traditional garden tools, plus topiary frames and herb dryers

Chasmood Shutters

Unit 8, Weydown Road Industrial Estate, Haslemere, Surrey
GU27 1DW
01428 641655

Traditional wooden shutters

Connoisseur Sun Dials

Lane's End, Strefford Craven Arms, Salop SY7 8DE
01588 672126

Sundials in brass and bronze

Country Crafts

The Willow Barn, Redburn, Hexham, Northumberland
NE47 7EA
01434 344453

Garden trellis arches, seats, arbours, compost bins and other garden furnishings and accessories

Cranborne Stone

West Orchard, Shaftesbury, Dorset SP7 0LJ
01258 472685

Stone planters, urns, benches, pergolas, statuary, balustrades and pond edgings

Dorset Weathervanes

284 Bournemouth Road, Charlton Marshall, Blandford Forum, Dorset DT11 9NG
01258 453374

Traditional and specialist weather-vane designs, including cars, walkers, fishermen and sailing boats. Also designs to commission

Elstead Lighting

Mill Lane, Alton, Hampshire GU34 2QG
01420 823777

Garden lighting

Filante Products

2 Watership Drive, Hightown, Ringwood, Hampshire BH24 1QY
01425 479409

Metal house name and number plaques

Freshfield Lane Brickworks

Danehill, Haywards Heath, Sussex RH17 7HH
01825 790350

Traditional paving stones, plus brick-built garden furniture

Garden Factory

Cannock Gates, Martindale Hawks Green, Cannock, Staffordshire WS11 2XT
01543 462500

Garden furniture and accessories

Gloster

Di-Scan UK, Concorde Road, Patchway, Bristol BS12 5TB
0117 9315335

Garden and conservatory furniture, including seats, chairs, tables, occasional pieces, cushions and parasols

Good Directions

Unit 15, Talisman Business Centre, Duncan Road, Park Gate, Southampton SO31 7GA
01489 577828

Traditional weather-vanes, cupolas and clock towers, sundials and decorative garden taps and door knockers

G W Thornton & Sons

Grether House, Crown Royal Industrial Park, Shawcross Street, Stockport, Cheshire SK1 3HB
0161 474 1525

Catalogue packed with garden tools, gadgets and some decorative products

Haddonstone

The Forge House, Church Lane, East Haddon, Northamptonshire NN6 8DB
01604 770711

Garden urns and ornaments, fountains and wall masks

Heritage Woodcraft

Unit 5, Shelley Farm, Ower, Nr Romsey, Hampshire SO51 6AS
01703 814145

Wooden furniture and traditional wood wheelbarrows

Hevengingham Collection

Weston Down, Weston Colley, Micheldever, Winchester, Hampshire SO21 3AQ
01962 774990

Wrought iron tables, chairs, trellises and planters in classical designs for gardens and conservatories

Holloways

Lower Court, Suckley, Worcestershire WR6 5DE
01886 884665

Large showroom packed with antique and contemporary garden ornaments, furniture and statuary

Homebase

Call 0645 801800 for your local store

Good range of pots, furniture and fencing, plus plants and accessories

Hortus Ornamenti

23 Cleveland Road, Chichester, West Sussex PO19 2HF
01243 782467

Hand-made garden tools and accessories, many based on Victorian designs. Mail order available

Imperial Stone

Rake Industries, Rake, Nr Petersfield, Hampshire GU31 5DR
01730 895382

Statuary, urns, fountains, finials and benches based on traditional designs and made in Portland or Bath stone finishes

Indian Ocean Trading Company

155–163 Balham Hill, London SW12 9DJ
0181 675 4808

Huge range of garden and outdoor dining furniture in teak and cast iron. Also supplies parasols with terracotta or stone bases

Jardinique

Kemps Place, Selborne Road, Greatham, Liss, Hampshire GU33 6HG
01420 538000

Antique and modern garden accessories and features

Juro Antiques

Whitbourne, Worcester WR6 5SF
01886 821261

Farm and garden antiques, including stone troughs, fountains, urns, bird baths and sundials

Kiln

20 Falconwood Court, Montpelier Row, London SE3 0RS
0181 463 0855

Ornamental pots from around the world

Letterbox Company

Tebworth, Leighton Buzzard, Bedfordshire LU7 9QG
01525 874599

Traditional letterboxes

Marshalls Mono

Southowram, Halifax HX3 9SY
01422 306000 (01422 306090 for brochures)

Paving products for pathways and drives, plus other landscape products

MC Products Ironcraft

Home Farm Cliffe, Piercebridge, Darlington, Co Durham
DL2 3SS
01325 374676

Iron gates and railings

Neptune Classics

Sevington Farm, Chippenham, Wiltshire SN14 7LD
01249 783252

Traditional tables, chairs, benches, hammocks and parasols. Fast mail-order delivery

Oxley's Furniture

01386 840466

Intricate aluminium outdoor and conservatory furniture

Paul Reef Parasols

Unit 6, Centre Park, Marston Business Park, Rudgate,
Tockwith, Yorkshire YO5 8QF
01423 358440

Parasols and teak garden furniture

Rayment Wirework

01843 821628

Wire hanging baskets, sculptures and garden furniture

Robinsons Greenhouses

Robinsons House, First Avenue, Millbrook, Southampton
SO15 0LG
01703 703355

Distinctive range of craftsman-built greenhouses, glasshouses, sun lounges and lean-tos

Ron Flynn

Call 01203 692981 for a brochure

Ornamental garden ironwork

Rusco Marketing

Little Farringdon Mill, Lechlade, Gloucestershire GL7 3QQ
01367 252754

Tree seats, benches and dining furniture in teak, iroko and wrought iron, plus planters, hammocks, cushions and parasols

Samson's

Gardenframes, Edwin Avenue, Hoo Farm Industrial Estate, Worcester Road, Kidderminster, Worcestershire DY11 7RA
01562 825201

Obelisks, frames, arches, trellises, pergolas and walkways

Stiffkey Lampshop

Stiffkey, Norfolk NR23 1AJ
01328 830460

Garden lighting

Stonemarket

Old Gravel Quarry, Oxford Road, Ryton on Dunsmore, Warwickshire CV8 3EJ
01203 305530

Garden paving, including Yorkstone cobbles, flags and millstones

Terrace & Garden

Call 01799 543289

Stylish garden and conservatory furniture in iron, bent cane and verdigris finishes by mail order

The Box Office

Thornbank House, Fore Street, Culmstock, Devon EX15 3JD
01884 840240

Wood and brass windowboxes made to order

The English Gardenwares Society

Tyrone House, Norton, Chichester PO20 6NH
01243 543804

Traditional gardening items

The London Decking Company

1 Dockhead Wharf, 4 Shad Thames, London SE1 2YT
0171 378 1061

Timber decking for outdoor eating areas

The Packhouse Antique Centre

Hewett's Kilns, Tongham Road, Runfold, Farnham, Surrey
GU10 1PQ
01252 783863

Garden antiques, as well as a huge range of old furniture

The Teak Tiger Trading Company

Broomfield House, Newton Green, Sudbury, Suffolk
CO10 0QS
01787 880900

Solid wood garden and conservatory furniture, including folding tables and chairs, loungers and benches

The Traditional Garden Supply Company

01483 273366

Garden catalogue packed with furniture, tools, compact greenhouses and tool stores, furniture and gifts

The Weather Store

72 Lapins Lane, Kings Hill, West Malling, Kent ME19 4LE
01732 848441

Weather-vanes in a large range of designs

Tobias & the Angel

68 White Hart Lane, London SW13 0PZ
0181 878 8902

Traditional gardening tools and paraphernalia

Touch Design

51 High Street, Sixpenny Handley, Salisbury, Wiltshire
SP5 5ND
01725 552888

Planters, trellises and other garden accessories

Vale Garden Houses

Call 01476 564433

Lightweight aluminium planters

Webbs Distribution

Unit 2, 15 Station Road, Knebworth, Hertfordshire SG3 6AP
01438 814620

Weather-vanes, planters, hanging baskets and brackets, plinths, pedestals and obelisks

Westwood Dials

White House Farm, New Hall Lane, Mundon, Essex CM9 6PJ
01621 740599

Decorative sundials

Whichford Pottery

Whichford, Nr Shipston-on-Stour, Warwickshire CV36 5PG
01608 684416

Garden pots and urns

Wickham Mercantile Company

Sunnybank Cottage, Arford Common, Headley, Bordon, Hampshire GU35 8AD
01420 474664

Benches, chairs and chaises-longues

Windrush Mill

01993 770456

Catalogue containing wide range of garden furniture and accessories

---

Calling in the Professionals

If you don't know where to start with your garden – either because it's a jungle or because it's an empty space – it could be worth getting advice from a professional. You need to have a clear idea of the basic elements you want to include (pond, outdoor eating area, vegetable patch, etc), and work out a budget before you start. Be realistic about the type of garden that will suit you – a designer can easily work out a scheme using low-maintenance and disease-resistant plants if you lack time or fall into the fair-weather gardener category! Contact the Society of Garden Designers, 6 Borough Road, Kingston upon Thames, Surrey KT2 6BD (0181 974 9483) for a useful booklet and details of members.

Conservatories

Amdega

Faverdale, Darlington, Durham DL3 0PW
01325 468522

Appeal Blinds

Call 0117 9637734

BAC

Edinburgh Drive, Eastern Avenue, Romford, Essex RM7 7PX
01708 745801

Bartholomew Conservatories

Haslemere Industrial Estate, Weydown Road, Haslemere, Surrey GU27 1DW
01428 658771

B&Q Conservatories

Portswood House, 1 Hampshire Corporate Park, Chandlers Ford, Eastleigh, Hants SO5 3YX
01703 256256

Conservatory Gardens

Call 0181 994 6109

C R Smith Conservatory

Call 01383 732181

Durabuild

Wheler Road, Coventry, West Midlands CV3 4LB
01203 639696

Grovewood Conservatory Blinds

Call 01332 544855

John Carr

Call 0800 591202 for brochures

Magnet Conservatories

Keighley, West Yorks BD21 4BY
01535 661133

Marston & Langinger

192 Ebury Street, London SW1W 8UP
0171 823 6829

Oak Leaf Conservatories

Kettlestring Lane, Clifton Moor, York YO3 4XF
01904 690401

Portland Conservatories

Park House Industrial Estate, Chesterton, Newcastle-under-Lyme ST5 7EF
0161 745 7920

Thomas Sanderson Blinds

Sanderson Buildings, Aston Road, Waterlooville, Hants PO7 7HT
01705 232600

The Conservatory Association

Call 0171 207 5873 for advice and listings of reputable firms

Town & Country Conservatories

Horningtoff, Dereham, Norfolk NR20 5DY
01328 700565

Vale Garden Houses

Melton Road, Harlaxton, Lincolnshire NG32 1HQ
01476 564433

Wessex Conservatories

Hawksworth, Swindon SN2 1D2
01793 644633

Wickes

120–138 Station Road, Harrow, Middx HA1 2QB
0181 863 5696

Space-making Designs

There are some really ingenious conservatory designs on the market – they've even been built on roof terraces. Planning permission is more likely to be required if the conservatory is above ground level, so do check with your local authority before work goes ahead. Custom-built designs tend to be more expensive than off-the-peg varieties, but they can still be a cost-effective way of creating an extra room.
